SCIENTIFIC RESEARCH IN EDUCATION

Committee on Scientific Principles for Education Research

Richard J. Shavelson and Lisa Towne, Editors

Center for Education
Division of Behavioral and Social Sciences and Education
National Research Council

National Academy Press
Washington, DC

NATIONAL ACADEMY PRESS • 2101 Constitution Avenue, NW • Washington, DC 20418

NOTICE: The project that is the subject of this report was approved by the Governing Board of the National Research Council, whose members are drawn from the councils of the National Academy of Sciences, the National Academy of Engineering, and the Institute of Medicine. The members of the committee responsible for the report were chosen for their special competences and with regard for appropriate balance.

This study was supported by Contract No. ED-00-00-0038 between the National Academy of Sciences and the U.S. Department of Education National Educational Research Policy and Priorities Board. Any opinions, findings, conclusions, or recommendations expressed in this publication are those of the author(s) and do not necessarily reflect the views of the organizations or agencies that provided support for the project.

Library of Congress Control Number 2002101615
International Standard Book Number 0-309-08291-9

Additional copies of this report are available from National Academy Press, 2101 Constitution Avenue, N.W., Lockbox 285, Washington, DC 20055; (800) 624-6242 or (202) 334-3313 (in the Washington metropolitan area); Internet, http://www.nap.edu

Suggested citation: National Research Council. (2002). *Scientific research in education.* Committee on Scientific Principles for Education Research. Shavelson, R.J., and Towne, L., Editors. Center for Education. Division of Behavioral and Social Sciences and Education. Washington, DC: National Academy Press.

First Printing, March 2002
Second Printing, August 2002
Third Printing, January 2003

THE NATIONAL ACADEMIES

National Academy of Sciences
National Academy of Engineering
Institute of Medicine
National Research Council

The **National Academy of Sciences** is a private, nonprofit, self-perpetuating society of distinguished scholars engaged in scientific and engineering research, dedicated to the furtherance of science and technology and to their use for the general welfare. Upon the authority of the charter granted to it by the Congress in 1863, the Academy has a mandate that requires it to advise the federal government on scientific and technical matters. Dr. Bruce M. Alberts is president of the National Academy of Sciences.

The **National Academy of Engineering** was established in 1964, under the charter of the National Academy of Sciences, as a parallel organization of outstanding engineers. It is autonomous in its administration and in the selection of its members, sharing with the National Academy of Sciences the responsibility for advising the federal government. The National Academy of Engineering also sponsors engineering programs aimed at meeting national needs, encourages education and research, and recognizes the superior achievements of engineers. Dr. Wm. A. Wulf is president of the National Academy of Engineering.

The **Institute of Medicine** was established in 1970 by the National Academy of Sciences to secure the services of eminent members of appropriate professions in the examination of policy matters pertaining to the health of the public. The Institute acts under the responsibility given to the National Academy of Sciences by its congressional charter to be an adviser to the federal government and, upon its own initiative, to identify issues of medical care, research, and education. Dr. Kenneth I. Shine is president of the Institute of Medicine.

The **National Research Council** was organized by the National Academy of Sciences in 1916 to associate the broad community of science and technology with the Academy's purposes of furthering knowledge and advising the federal government. Functioning in accordance with general policies determined by the Academy, the Council has become the principal operating agency of both the National Academy of Sciences and the National Academy of Engineering in providing services to the government, the public, and the scientific and engineering communities. The Council is administered jointly by both Academies and the Institute of Medicine. Dr. Bruce M. Alberts and Dr. Wm. A. Wulf are chairman and vice chairman, respectively, of the National Research Council.

Dedication

Lee J. Cronbach (1916-2001)

Lee Cronbach was the Vida Jacks Professor of Education Emeritus at Stanford University and member of the National Academy of Sciences and the National Academy of Education. His career spanned five decades and yielded seminal contributions to psychometrics, instruction, and program evaluation. His ideas and high standards for rigorous scientific inquiry greatly influenced educational and social science research and the deliberations of our committee.

Foreword

The National Academies have been in the business of bringing science to bear on pressing problems since 1863. Our operating arm—the National Research Council (NRC)—has produced hundreds of reports that synthesize scientific knowledge in a wide range of areas that affect the public interest. Most of this work involves scientists acting to promote rational decision making in matters of public policy. Less often, our reports explicitly comment on the nature of the scientific enterprise itself. This report is such an example. Its authoring committee was assembled amid vibrant debate about quality and rigor in scientific education research. In the course of its work, the committee revisited long-standing philosophies about the nature of science, so as to place them in the context of modern education research.

Because in many ways this report is itself a product of scientific work, it had to live up to its own depiction of what constitutes good science. The authoring committee has applied rigorous reasoning to its scrutiny of evidence and ideas, considered alternative perspectives, and presented its findings and conclusions in a language that invites constructive discussion.

I hope that *Scientific Research in Education* will advance the current dialogue in at least two respects. First, it offers a comprehensive perspective of "scientifically-based" education research for the policy communities who are increasingly interested in its utilization for improving education policy and practice. Second, the report shows that, within the diverse field of education, researchers who often disagree along philosophical and methodological lines nonetheless share much common ground about the definition and pursuit of quality. This report should therefore be useful for researchers, as well as for those who use research.

This effort continues a series of recent institutional changes and initiatives within the NRC designed to elevate the role of education research in improving policy and practice. In 1999, we created the Center for Education to integrate and strengthen our already substantial portfolio of work in education and education research. In addition, a major NRC initiative called the Strategic Education Research Partnership focuses on developing the capacity and infrastructure to systematically link education research and practice. Taken together, these and future efforts are intended to help transform education into an increasingly evidence-based field—one of the most important goals of my presidency.

Like any good scholarly work, this book will no doubt incite debate and discussion, invite critique and commentary, and claim its defenders and detractors. As the authors argue in the pages that follow, this kind of professional, constructive discourse is precisely what characterizes a healthy scientific community. We welcome the dialogue to come.

Bruce Alberts
President, National Academy of Sciences

Acknowledgments

This report could not have been produced without support from a number of people, and the committee is grateful for their contributions. First, we wish to acknowledge our sponsor, the U.S. Department of Education's National Educational Research Policy and Priorities Board, and in particular Kenji Hakuta, Thelma Leenhouts, Mary Grace Lucier, Alba Ortiz, and Rafael Valdivieso.

The committee was aided greatly by individuals who participated in our meetings and helped us understand the complex issues involved in examining the nature of scientific inquiry in education. At our first meeting in December 2000, Tom Glennan of RAND, Jane Oates of the office of U.S. Senator Kennedy, D'Arcy Philps formerly of the Committee on Education and the Workforce of the U.S. House of Representatives, and Alexandra (Sandy) Wigdor of the National Research Council all provided helpful presentations about the context of our work.

In March 2001 the committee hosted a workshop on science, evidence, and inference in education. We are particularly grateful for the contributions of the workshop speakers and panelists: Michael Agar, University of Maryland and Ethknoworks; Norman Bradburn, U.S. National Science Foundation; Glen Cain, University of Wisconsin; Susan Chipman, U.S. Office of Naval Research; Christopher T. Cross, Council for Basic Education; Larry Hedges, University of Chicago; Jeremy Kilpatrick, University of Georgia; David Klahr, Carnegie Mellon University; Sharon Lewis, Council of Great City Schools; Reid Lyon, U.S. National Institute of Child Heath and Human Development; Kent McGuire, Manpower Demonstration Research Corporation; Robert Mislevy, University of Maryland; William Morrill, Caliber Associates; William Quinn, North Central Regional Educational Laboratory; Diane Ravitch, New York University and Brookings Institution; Sally Rockey, Cooperative State Research, Education, and Extension Service, U.S. Department of Agriculture; Steven Ross, University of Memphis; Nancy Songer, University of Michigan; Judith Sunley, U.S. National Science Foundation; Richard Suzman, U.S. National Institute on Aging; Peter Tillers, Cardozo Law School, Yeshiva University, and Yale Law School; and Maris Vinovskis, University of Michigan. We also want to thank all of the workshop participants, whose active engagement over the course of the 2-day workshop significantly enhanced the dialogue.

In the months following the workshop, Norman Bradburn, Reid Lyon, Judith Sunley, and Richard Suzman continued to be of tremendous assistance as we collected more data on the research activities of their federal agencies. Special thanks go to Martin Orland at the U.S. Department of Education's Office of Educational Research and Improvement; his help in the development of our data collection instrument was invaluable, as were the extensive data he provided.

The committee also benefited from discussion with and ideas from several National Academy of Sciences and Institute of Medicine members during our deliberations: Arthur Goldberger, Eleanor Maccoby, James March, Neil Smelser, and Patrick Suppes. Their willingness to share their insights with the committee at a formative time of our deliberations was extraordinarily generous.

Many others have supported this project. The staff at the library and archives of the Educational Testing Service provided considerable assistance in putting together the material on the history of assessment. Several staff members at the National Research Council (NRC) Center for Education provided informal guidance to staff throughout the entire process, especially Naomi Chudowsky. The center's director, Michael Feuer, was very generous of his time; his advice throughout the course of this project was invaluable. We also wish to thank Kirsten Sampson Snyder for guiding us through the report review process and Eugenia Grohman for her expert editing of the manuscript. The committee is especially grateful for the project staff support of Linda DePugh, who provided logistical and administrative assistance throughout the project, and Tina Winters, who managed the post-workshop data collection and provided assistance with manuscript preparation. Their contributions were essential to producing this volume.

This report has been reviewed in draft form by individuals chosen for their diverse perspectives and technical expertise, in accordance with procedures approved by the NRC's Report Review Committee. The purpose of this independent review is to provide candid and critical comments that will assist the institution in making its published report as sound as possible and to ensure that the report meets institutional standards for objectivity, evidence, and responsiveness to the study charge. The review comments and draft manuscript remain confidential to protect the integrity of the deliberative process. We wish to thank the following individuals for their review of this report: Deborah Lowenberg Ball, University of Michigan; Hyman Bass, University of Michigan; M. Susan Burns, George Mason University; Thomas Cook, Northwestern University; David S. Cordray, Vanderbilt University; Michael Doyle, Research Corporation; James Duderstadt, University of Michigan; Arthur S. Goldberger, University of Wisconsin-Madison; Jane Hannaway, The Urban Institute; William Reese, University of Wisconsin-Madison; Marshall Smith, William and Flora Hewlett Foundation; and John Willinsky, University of British Columbia.

Although the reviewers listed above have provided many constructive comments and suggestions, they were not asked to endorse the conclusions or recommendations nor did they see the final draft of the report before its release. The review of this report was overseen by Robert L. Linn, University of Colorado, and Lyle V. Jones, The University of North Carolina at Chapel Hill. Appointed by the NRC, they were responsible for making certain that an independent examination of this report was carried out in accordance with institutional procedures and that all review comments were carefully considered. Responsibility for the final content of this report rests entirely with the authoring committee and the institution.

Finally, we must thank the members of our marvelous committee. It was no small task to agree on and articulate the nature of scientific research in education, particularly in less than a year's time. It was their dedication, perseverance, and collective expertise that made it possible. And it was their candid, professional approach that made the effort rewarding and fun.

Richard J. Shavelson, *Chair*
Lisa Towne, *Study Director*

Contents

SCIENTIFIC RESEARCH IN
EDUCATION

Executive Summary

N o one would think of getting to the Moon or of wiping out a disease without research. Likewise, one cannot expect reform efforts in education to have significant effects without research-based knowledge to guide them. Scientific research in education can shed light on the increasingly complex and performance-driven U.S. education system. Such research covers a wide range of issues, including teaching second-language learners, measurement of achievement and self-concept, the biological and psychological basis of language and cognition, public school finance, and postsecondary and life-long learning outcomes.

There is long-standing debate among scholars, policy makers, and others about the nature and value of scientific research in education and the extent to which it has produced the kind of cumulative knowledge expected of scientific endeavors. Most recently, this skepticism led to proposed legislation that defines what constitutes rigorous scientific methods for conducting education research.

That proposal, coupled with rising enthusiasm for evidence-based education policy and practice, led to this National Research Council study to examine and clarify the nature of scientific inquiry in education and how the federal government can best foster and support it. Specifically, the charge to the committee was to "...review and synthesize recent literature on the science and practice of scientific educational research and consider how to support high quality science in a federal education research agency." We did not attempt to evaluate the quality of bodies of existing research, of existing researchers in the field, or of the existing federal research function because that would have constituted a monumental challenge and we judged it to be beyond the scope of our charge. Instead, we adopted a forward-looking approach that draws on lessons from history and identifies the roles of various stakeholders (e.g., researchers, policy makers, practitioners) in fulfilling a vision for the future of education research.

NATURE OF SCIENCE

At its core, scientific inquiry is the same in all fields. Scientific research, whether in education, physics, anthropology, molecular biology, or economics, is a continual process of rigorous reasoning supported by a dynamic interplay among methods, theories, and findings. It builds understandings in the form of models or theories that can be tested. Advances in scientific knowledge are achieved by the self-regulating norms of the scientific community over time, not, as sometimes believed, by the mechanistic application of a particular scientific method to a static set of questions.

The accumulation of scientific knowledge over time is circuitous and indirect. It often traverses highly contested territory—by researchers and other interested parties—and progresses as a result of a not-so-invisible hand of professional skepticism and criticism. Rarely does one study produce an unequivocal and durable result; multiple methods, applied over time and tied to evidentiary standards, are essential to establishing a base of scientific knowledge. Formal syntheses of research findings across studies are often necessary to discover, test, and explain the diversity of findings that characterize many fields. And it takes time to build scientific knowledge, whether in the physical, life, and social sciences or in areas related to education.

The scientific enterprise depends on a healthy community of researchers and is guided by a set of fundamental principles. These principles are not a set of rigid standards for conducting and evaluating individual studies, but rather are a set of norms enforced by the community of researchers that shape scientific understanding. We conclude that six guiding principles underlie all scientific inquiry, including education research:

SCIENTIFIC PRINCIPLE 1
Pose Significant Questions That Can Be Investigated Empirically

Moving from hunch to conceptualizing and specifying a worthwhile question is essential to scientific research. Questions are posed in an effort to fill a gap in existing knowledge or to seek new knowledge, to pursue the identification of the cause or causes of some phenomena, or to formally test a hypothesis. Ultimately, the final court of appeal for the viability of a scientific hypothesis or conjecture is its empirical adequacy. Scientists and philosophers commonly hold that the testability and refutability of scientific claims or hypotheses is an important feature of scientific investigations that is not typical in other forms of inquiry. The questions, and the designs developed to address them, must reflect a solid understanding of the relevant theoretical, methodological, and empirical work that has come before.

SCIENTIFIC PRINCIPLE 2
Link Research to Relevant Theory

It is the long-term goal of much of science to generate theories that can offer stable explanations for phenomena that generalize beyond the particular. Every scientific inquiry is linked, either implicitly or explicitly, to some overarching theory or conceptual framework that guides the entire investigation. Science generates cumulative knowledge by building on, refining, and occasionally replacing, theoretical understanding.

SCIENTIFIC PRINCIPLE 3
Use Methods That Permit Direct Investigation of the Question

Methods can only be judged in terms of their appropriateness and effectiveness in addressing a particular research question. Moreover, scientific claims are significantly strengthened when they are subject to testing by multiple methods. While appropriate methodology is important for individual studies, it also has a larger aspect. Particular research designs and methods are suited for specific kinds of investigations and questions, but can rarely illuminate all the questions and issues in a line of inquiry. Therefore, very different methodological approaches must often be used in various parts of a series of related studies.

SCIENTIFIC PRINCIPLE 4
Provide a Coherent and Explicit Chain of Reasoning

At the core of science is inferential reasoning: explanations, conclusions, or predictions based on what is known and observed. Making scientific inferences is not accomplished by merely applying an algorithm for using accepted techniques in correct ways. Rather, it requires the development of a logical chain of reasoning from evidence to theory and back again that is coherent, shareable, and persuasive to the skeptical reader. The validity of inferences made through this process is strengthened by identifying limitations and biases, estimating uncertainty and error, and, crucially, systematically ruling out plausible counterexplanations in a rational, compelling way. Detailed descriptions of procedures and analyses are critical to permit others to critique, to analyze, and to attempt to replicate, a study.

SCIENTIFIC PRINCIPLE 5
Replicate and Generalize Across Studies

Scientific inquiry emphasizes checking and validating individual findings and results. Since all studies rely on a limited set of observations, a key question is how individual findings generalize to broader populations and settings. Ultimately, scientific knowledge advances when findings are reproduced in a range of times and places and when findings are integrated and synthesized.

SCIENTIFIC PRINCIPLE 6
Disclose Research to Encourage Professional Scrutiny and Critique

Scientific studies do not contribute to a larger body of knowledge until they are widely disseminated and subjected to professional scrutiny by peers. This ongoing, collaborative, public critique is an indication of the health of a scientific enterprise. Indeed, the objectivity of science derives from publicly enforced norms of the professional community of scientists, rather than from the character traits of any individual person or design features of any study.

APPLICATION OF THE PRINCIPLES TO EDUCATION

While all sciences share common principles, every field of study develops a specialization as the principles are applied. Education has its own set of features—not individually unique from other professional and disciplinary fields of study, but singular in their combination—that gives rise to the specialization of education research.

Education is multilayered, constantly shifting, and occurs within an interaction among institutions (e.g., schools and universities), communities, and families. It is highly value laden and involves a diverse array of people and political forces that significantly shapes its character. These features require attention to the physical, social, cultural, economic, and historical environment in the research process because these contextual factors often influence results in significant ways. Because the U.S. education system is so heterogeneous and the nature of teaching and learning so complex, attention to context is especially critical for understanding the extent to which theories and findings may generalize to other times, places, and populations.

Education research as a profession has defining features as well. For example, multiple disciplinary perspectives bear on the study of education. Furthermore, conducting education research that involves studying humans (e.g., students, teachers) is governed by the need to ensure ethical treatment of these participants. Finally, education research depends on its relationships with practice. These links exist along a spectrum: some types of research require only a weak connection; others require full partnerships with schools or other entities. In order to analyze state assessment data, parents and schools have to agree to a test administration. To study mechanisms by which interventions increase student achievement would require long-term partnerships between research and practice.

The features of education, in combination with the guiding principles of science, set the boundaries for the design of scientific education research. The design of a study does not make the study scientific. A wide variety of legitimate scientific designs are available for education research. They range from randomized experiments of voucher programs to in-depth ethnographic case studies of teachers to neurocognitive investigations of number learning using positive emission tomography brain imaging. To be scientific, the design must allow direct, empirical investigation of an important question, account for the context in which the study is carried out, align with a conceptual framework, reflect careful and thorough reasoning, and disclose results to encourage debate in the scientific community.

DESIGN PRINCIPLES FOR FOSTERING SCIENCE IN A FEDERAL EDUCATION RESEARCH AGENCY

How should a federal education research agency be designed if the goal is to foster scientific research on education, given the complexities of the practice of education, the stringencies of the scientific principles, and the wide range of legitimate research designs? To address this question, we did not conduct an evaluation of the Office of Educational Research and Improvement (OERI), the chief existing research agency in the U.S. Department of Education. Moreover, the committee was not charged with, nor did we attempt to develop, a comprehensive blueprint for federal education research agency; that work is best left to organizational design experts and the political process. Rather, the committee developed six design principles for a federal education research agency to nurture a *scientific culture* within the agency. The precise structure itself is not the critical element. The committee's review of the processes and practices across a range of federal research agencies and of the history of the education research agency in particular suggests that it is not the nuts and bolts of agency mechanics that differentiates successful agencies from unsuccessful ones; agencies are effective when their culture supports the principles of science.

To develop such a scientific culture, the agency must have an infrastructure that is insulated from political micromanagement, supported by sufficient and sustained resources, and led by staff with top scientific and management credentials who have the flexibility to make decisions and are accountable for them. Importantly, responsibility for the success of such an agency lies with all education stakeholders. The government cannot mandate a healthy federal role. In particular, the community of education researchers—as a matter of professional responsibility—must engage in its work to promote the agency's critical role in a vibrant education research enterprise. The design principles that follow elaborate these core ideas and include suggestions for supporting mechanisms.

DESIGN PRINCIPLE 1
Staff the Agency with People Skilled in Science, Leadership, and Management

The director of the agency should have demonstrated outstanding leadership capabilities and be a respected researcher in education. Research staff should hold similar qualifications, as well as be adept at writing grant announcements, engaging with the field to identify research gaps and priorities, and assembling panels of peers to perform various tasks. Qualified staff is so critical to a healthy agency that we believe without them, little else matters. Only with such staff can the norms of scientific research in education become infused into the agency.

DESIGN PRINCIPLE 2
Create Structures to Guide the Research Agenda, Inform Funding Decisions, and Monitor Work

The research agenda must be developed through a collaborative process that engages the range of stakeholders in education. An advisory board of researchers, practitioners, business people, and policy makers (perhaps modeled after the National Science Board) could work in collaboration with an agenda-setting committee. To provide additional input to the agenda-setting process, as well as to vet research proposals, peer review is the single best, although certainly not perfect, model. Standing peer-review panels, preferably with rotating terms, can learn from, and communicate to, the field and in turn be especially strong instruments for promoting scientific progress over time. The choice of peers with excellent scientific credentials and an ability to think across areas is the key to making this commonly used mechanism work, and depends critically on an ample talent pool of peers.

DESIGN PRINCIPLE 3
Insulate the Agency from Inappropriate Political Interference

The research agency must be insulated from political micromanagement, the distortion of research agendas by excessive focus on immediate problems, and the use of the agency as a tool to promote particular policies or positions. At the same time, its work should include policy research and short-term work that is responsive to current priorities and needs. Given trends in "hybrid" federal organizations that support both education research and service-oriented programs, we suggest that the research function of an agency be organizationally separate from, though intellectually linked to, an educational improvement mission to ensure that the research mission is nurtured.

DESIGN PRINCIPLE 4
Develop a Focused and Balanced Portfolio of Research That Addresses Short-, Medium-, and Long-term Issues of Importance to Policy and Practice

Short- and medium-term scientific studies are most responsive to the need for answers to questions of pressing problems of practice and policy. Long-term studies address fundamental questions by focusing on the development and testing of theoretical frameworks. All should be organized in coherent programs of related work. The portfolio should include research syntheses as well as new scientific investigations.

DESIGN PRINCIPLE 5
Adequately Fund the Agency

Estimates of the federal investment in education research have shown it to be a few tenths of one percent of the total amount spent on public elementary and secondary education each year—far less than comparable investments for agriculture and medicine. The research budget of the OERI (and its predecessor agency, the National Institute of Education) has fallen drastically since its inception: in 1973, its budget was over $525 million; today, it is approximately $130 million (both in 2000 dollars). As funding plummeted, there has been no commensurate change in the scope of its agenda, and thus there have been few opportunities for long-term research programs. We echo the calls of several previous studies and commissions for a significantly increased research budget if its agenda is to cover the breadth of content required of its predecessors. Stagnant funding, an inconsistent commitment, or both, means that scientific research in education is not being taken seriously.

DESIGN PRINCIPLE 6
Invest in Research Infrastructure

The agency should consistently invest in infrastructure-building programs to foster a scientifically competent, highly qualified community of education researchers and to strengthen its own capacity in turn. Since an agency in many ways is a reflection of the field it supports, such programs should include investment in human capital (e.g., research training and fellowship support). Promoting ethical access to research subjects and data should be an essential task as well. An agency should also do its part to facilitate relationships between practitioners and researchers both for basic access to data as well as, in many field-based research efforts, for long-term partnerships with practitioner communities to improve the research as well as its utilization.

1

Introduction

Born of egalitarian instincts, the grand experiment of U.S. public education began over 200 years ago. The scope and complexity of its agenda is apparent:

to teach the fundamental skills of reading, writing, and arithmetic; to nurture critical thinking; to convey a general fund of knowledge; to develop creativity and aesthetic perception; to assist students in choosing and preparing for vocations in a highly complex economy; to inculcate ethical character and good citizenship; to develop physical and emotional well-being; and to nurture the ability, the intelligence, and the will to continue on with education as far as any particular individual wants to go (Cremin, 1990, p. 42).

The educational system is no less complex. Today the United States sends more than 45 million children to schools that are governed by 15,000 independent school districts in the 50 states (and territories); it boasts thousands of colleges and universities and myriad adult and informal learning centers. The nation takes pride in reaffirming the constitutional limitations on the federal role in education, yet recently has tentatively embraced the idea of national standards. The system is one of dualities: a national ethos with local control; commitment to excellence and aspiration to equality; and faith in tradition and appetite for innovation.

The context in which this system operates is also changing. The United States is no longer a manufacturing society in which people with little formal education can find moderate- to high-paying jobs. It is now a service- and knowledge-driven economy in which high levels of literacy and numeracy are required of almost everyone to achieve a good standard of living (National Research Council, 1999a; Secretary's Commission on Achieving Necessary Skills, 1991; Murnane and Levy, 1996; Judy and D'Amico, 1997; Packer, 1997). Moreover, to address the challenges of, for example, low-performing schools, the "achievement gap," and language diversity, educators today require new knowledge to reengineer schools in effective ways.

To meet these new demands, rigorous, sustained, scientific research in education is needed. In today's rapidly changing economic and techno-logical environment, schooling cannot be improved by relying on folk wisdom about how students learn and how schools should be organized. No one would think of designing a rocket to the moon or wiping out a widespread disease by relying on untested hunches; likewise, one cannot expect to improve education without research.

Knowledge is needed on many topics, including: how to motivate children to succeed; how effective schools and classrooms are organized to foster learning; the roots of teenage alienation and violence; how human and economic resources can be used to support effective instruction; effec-tive strategies for preparing teachers and school administrators; the inter-action among what children learn in the context of their families, schools, colleges, and the media; the relationship between educational policy and the economic development of society; and the ways that the effects of schooling are moderated by culture and language. In order that society can learn how to improve its efforts to mount effective programs, rigorous evaluations of innovations must also be conducted. The education research community has produced important insights on many of these topics (we trace some of them in Chapter 2). However, in contrast to physics and other older sciences, many areas of education are relatively new domains for scientific study, and there is much work yet to do.

Everyone has opinions about schooling, because they were all once in school. But in this ever more complex world, in which educational prob-lems tend to be portrayed with the urgency of national survival, there is (again) an understandable attraction to the rationality and disciplined style of science. Simply put, for some problems citizens, educators, administrators, policy makers, and other concerned individuals want to hear about hard evidence, they want impartiality, and they want decisions to rest on reasonable, rigorous, and scientific deliberation. And how can the quality of science be judged? This is our topic.

To set the stage for this discussion, this chapter provides historical and philosophical background and describes how the current undertaking fits into that broader context.

HISTORICAL AND PHILOSOPHICAL CONTEXT

Education research in the United States is barely 100 years old, and its history is not a simple tale of progress. The study of education drew heavily on the emerging social sciences, which had found a place in research universities at the beginning of the twentieth century. That foothold was often tenuous, however, with intense debates about the essential character of these "sciences." Many in academic circles sought to model the social sciences on the physical sciences, while others—regarding this as "physics envy"—insisted that broader accounts of the nature of science had to be adopted in order to encompass adequately the range of phenomena in these newer domains (Lagemann, 2000).

Education research began as a branch of psychology at a time when psychology was still a part of philosophy. In the first decade of the twentieth century, psychology was emerging as a distinct field, as were the budding fields of educational psychology, history of education, and educational administration. By the 1930s, subfields of work that centered on different subjects of the school curriculum—notably reading, mathematics, and social studies—had also emerged. As education research continued to develop new methods and questions and in response to developments in the social and behavioral sciences, research fields proliferated (Lagemann, 2000; Cronbach and Suppes, 1969).

From the beginning, the field has been plagued by skepticism concerning the value and validity of developing a "science of education." This attitude was evident as long ago as the late nineteenth century, when universities began to establish departments and schools of education. A chorus of complaints arose from faculty in the arts and sciences concerning the inclusion of scholars intending to systematically study the organizational and pedagogical aspects of schooling. Ellwood Patterson Cubberley, a school superintendent in San Diego who just before the end of the nineteenth century was appointed chair of the department of education (later the School of Education) at Stanford University, arrived on campus ready and eager to help improve education by generating studies of the history and current administration of the nation's public schools. Despite his enthusiasm and extraordinary productivity, his colleagues refused to acknowledge that "the study of education could be validly considered either an art or a science." On the opposite side of the country Paul Hanus, Harvard's first scholar of education, faced similar skepticism. George Herbert Palmer liked to quip that when "Professor Hanus came to Cambridge, he bore the onus of his subject." (quoted in Lagemann, 2000, p. 72). Indeed, a set of attitudes toward education research that one might call "anti-educationism" has been a constant to the present day.

Despite this skepticism, the enterprise grew apace. For example, by the end of the twentieth century, the American Educational Research Association (AERA) had well over 20,000 members (roughly 5,500 of whom report research as their primary professional responsibility), organized into 12 divisions (e.g., administration, curriculum, learning and instruction, teacher education), some with a number of subsections, and about 140 special interest groups (American Educational Research Association, 2000). This growth in the number of scholars has been notable because it occurred in the absence of a proportional increase in federal funding. And as a percentage of the total amount spent on public elementary and secondary education, the nation as a whole invested less than 0.1 percent in research (President's Committee of Advisors on Science and Technology, 1997).

There are several reasons for the lack of public support for education research. Problems include research quality (Lagemann, 2000; Kaestle, 1993; Sroufe, 1997; Levin and O'Donnell, 1999), fragmentation of the effort (National Research Council, 1992), and oversimplified expectations about the role of research in education reform (National Research Council, 2001d). Another key problem has been the sharp divide between education research and scholarship and the practice of education in schools and other settings. This disconnect has several historic roots: researchers and practitioners have typically worked in different settings; most researchers have been men, while most teachers have been women; and teacher education has typically relied on practical experience rather than research. Operating in different worlds, researchers and practitioners did not develop the kinds of cross fertilization that are necessary in fields where research and practice should develop reciprocally—medicine and agriculture faced similar problems in their early development (Lagemann, 2000; Mitchell and Haro, 1999).

The epistemology of education research—that is, understanding about its core nature as a scientific endeavor—has also evolved significantly since its early days (see Dewey [1929] for an insightful early treatment). Five dimensions are particularly relevant to this report: the emergence of refined models of human nature; progress in understanding how scientific knowledge accumulates; recognition that education is a contested field of study; new developments in research designs and methods; and increased understanding of the nature of scientific rigor or quality. We comment briefly on each below and expand on several of them in the remaining chapters.

Models of Human Nature

In the decades when scientific research in education was gathering momentum, the most prevalent "models of man" and of human social life were derived from the mechanistic, positivistic sciences and philosophy of the nineteenth and twentieth centuries. The most famous example—the focus of numerous theoretical and methodological battles—was B.F. Skinner's behaviorism (Skinner, 1953/1965, 1972). Following the work of the logical positivist philosophers, who believed that talking about entities that were not available for direct inspection (such as thoughts, values, ideals, and beliefs) was literally meaningless, Skinner's research assumed that human behavior could be explained completely in terms of observable causes—for example, through schedules of reinforcement and punishment. Although Skinner's work laid the foundation for modern theories of behavior (see National Research Council, 2001b), the behaviorist paradigm excluded important phenomena from inquiry at the outset of the study. Today, it is recognized that many phenomena of interest across the domains of the social sciences and education research result from voluntary human actions (or from the unintended or aggregate consequences of such actions) even though direct measurement of such phenomena is typically not possible.[1] Thus, research on human action must take into account individuals' understandings, intentions, and values as well as their observable behavior (Phillips and Burbules, 2000; Phillips, 2000.)

The development of alternative perspectives on the nature of humans that are more inclusive than the once-dominant behaviorist perspective should be regarded as both highly promising and something of a cautionary tale for education research. The moral of the rise and at least partial fall of behaviorism warns the scientific community to resist the tendency to take a single model (whether behavioral, cognitive, or interpretive), derived in relation to a limited range of phenomena, and extrapolate it as appropriate across all the social and behavioral sciences. There is room in the mansion of science for more than one model, and also for the creative tension produced when rival models are deployed (see, for an example, Greeno et al., 1996).

Progress in Science

If appreciation for multiple perspectives on the nature of humans has enhanced efforts to develop scientific research, so has a better, more sophisticated awareness of what "progress" in science means and how it is achieved. Linear models of progress have been put aside in favor of more jagged ones. Mistakes are made as science moves forward. The process is not infallible (see Lakatos and Musgrave, 1970); science advances through professional criticism and self-correction. Indeed, we show in Chapter 2 that this jagged progression of scientific progress is typical across the range of physical and social sciences as well as education research.

A long history of the philosophy of science also teaches that there is no algorithm for scientific progress (and, consequently, we certainly do not attempt to offer one in this report). Despite its optimistic-sounding title, even Sir Karl Popper's (1959) classic work, *The Logic of Scientific Discovery*, makes the point strongly that there is no logical process by which researchers

---

[1]For example, car purchases—a result of human actions—are easily observable and trackable; however, the reasons that people purchase a particular brand at a particular time and in a particular place are not.

can make discoveries in the first place. Popper also argues that knowledge always remains conjectural and potentially revisable. Over time, erroneous theories and inaccurate findings are detected and eliminated, largely by the process of testing (seeking refutations) that Popper himself described (Popper, 1965; Newton-Smith, 1981).

Education—A Highly Contested Field

While knowledge in the physical and social sciences and education has accumulated over time, the highly contested nature of education has had an effect on the progress of scientific research (Lagemann, 1996). One reason education is highly contested is because values play a central role: people's hopes and expectations for educating the nation's young are integrally tied to their hopes and expectations about the direction of society and its development (Hirst and Peters, 1970; Dewey, 1916). Obviously, different people see these matters differently. As in other fields that have such a public character, social ideals inevitably influence the research that is done, the way it is framed and conducted, and the policies and practices that are based on research findings. And decisions about education are sometimes instituted with no scientific basis at all, but rather are derived directly from ideology or deeply held beliefs about social justice or the good of society in general.

A second reason that education is contested is that rarely, if ever, does an education intervention—one important focus of study in the broader domain of education research—have only one main effect. Both positive and negative unintended consequences are often important (Cronbach et al., 1980). Education interventions have costs—in money, time, and effort: making a judgment on the effectiveness of a treatment is complex and requires taking account of myriad factors.

In short, education research will inevitably reflect and have to face many different values, and it will as a consequence produce complex findings. Ultimately, policy makers and practicing educators will have to formulate specific policies and practices on the basis of values and practical wisdom as well as education research. Science-based education research will affect, but typically not solely determine, these policies and practices.

Research Design and Method

Research in education has been enhanced by the recent invention of methods: new observational techniques, new experimental designs, new methods of data gathering and analysis, and new software packages for managing and analyzing both quantitative and qualitative data. Rapid advances in computer technologies have also dramatically increased the capacity to store and analyze large data sets. As new methods are developed, they lead to the identification of new questions, and the investigation of these, in turn, can demand that new methods be devised. We illustrate this dynamic relationship between methods, theories, empirical findings, and problems in Chapter 2 and describe common designs and methods employed to address classes of research questions in Chapter 5.

Scientific Evidence and Rigor

In thinking about the ways that a research conjecture or hypothesis may be supported by evidence, many philosophers of science have found it fruitful to adopt a term that was featured in John Dewey's (1938) treatise, *Logic: The Theory of Inquiry* (see, e.g., Phillips and Burbules, 2000). Dewey wrote of *warrants* for making assertions or knowledge claims. In science, measurements and experimental results, observational or interview data, and mathematical and logical analysis all can be part of the warrant—or case—that supports a theory, hypothesis, or judgment. However, warrants are always revocable depending on the findings of subsequent inquiry. Beliefs that are strongly warranted or supported at one time (e.g., the geocentric model of the solar system) may later need to be abandoned (for a heliocentric model). Evidence that is regarded as authoritative at one time (e.g., ice ages are caused by the eccentricity of the Earth's orbit) can be shown later to be faulty (see Chapter 3). Science progresses both by advancing new theories or hypotheses and by eliminating theories, hypotheses, or previously accepted facts that have been refuted by newly acquired evidence judged to be definitive.

To make progress possible, then, theories, hypotheses, or conjectures must be stated in clear, unambiguous, and empirically testable terms. Evidence must be linked to them through a clear chain of reasoning. Moreover, the community of inquirers must be, in Karl Popper's expression, "open societies" that encourage the free flow of critical comment. Researchers have an obligation to avoid seeking only such evidence that apparently supports their favored hypotheses; they also must seek evidence that is incompatible with these hypotheses even if such evidence, when found, would refute their ideas. Thus, it is the scientific *community* that enables scientific progress, not, as Nobel Prize-winning physicist Polykarp Kusch once declared, adherence to any one scientific *method* (Mills, 2000 [emphasis added]). We emphasize this notion of community in the scientific enterprise throughout this report.

These points about the nature of evidence constitute the essence of our account of rigor in inquiry; these ideas are fleshed out in the rest of this report. Importantly, our vision of scientific quality and rigor applies to the two forms of education research that have traditionally been labeled "quantitative" and "qualitative," as well as to two forms of research that have been labeled "basic" and "applied." These dichotomies have historically formed fault lines within and outside academia. As our brief discussion of the emergence of schools of education suggests, the perceived hierarchy of basic or "pure" science versus its messier cousin—applied research—has isolated the field of education research from other sciences. Similarly, sharp distinctions between quantitative and qualitative inquiry have divided the field. In particular, the current trend of schools of education to favor qualitative methods, often at the expense of quantitative methods, has invited criticism. Real problems stem from these "either/or" kinds of preferences, and we believe that both categorizations are neither well defined nor constructive. Thus, beyond a brief discussion that follows, we do not dwell on them in the report.

It is common to see quantitative and qualitative methods described as being fundamentally different modes of inquiry—even as being different paradigms embodying quite different epistemologies (Howe, 1988; Phillips, 1987). We regard this view as mistaken. Because we see quantitative and qualitative scientific inquiry as being epistemologically quite similar (King, Keohane, and Verba, 1994; Howe and Eisenhart, 1990), and as we recognize that both can be pursued rigorously, we do not distinguish between them as being different forms of inquiry. We believe the distinction is outmoded, and it does not map neatly in a one-to-one fashion onto any group or groupings of disciplines.

We also believe the distinction between basic and applied science has outlived its usefulness. This distinction often served to denigrate applied work (into which category education research was usually placed). But as Stokes (1997) in *Pasteur's Quadrant* made clear, great scientific work has often been inspired by the desire to solve a pressing practical problem—much of the cutting-edge work of the scientist who inspired the book's title had this origin. What makes research scientific is not the motive for carrying it out, but the manner in which it is carried out.

Finally, it is important to note that the question of what constitutes scientific rigor and quality has been the topic of much debate within the education research community itself since the nineteenth century. Two extreme views in the field's complex history are worthy of brief elaboration. First, some extreme "postmodernists" have questioned whether there is any value in scientific evidence in education whatsoever (see the discussion of these issues in Gross, Levitt, and Lewis, 1997). At the other end of the spectrum, there are those who would define scientific research in education quite narrowly, suggesting that it is only quantitative measures and tight controls that unambiguously define science (see, e.g., Finn, 2001). We do not believe that either view is constructive, and in our estimation they have both compounded the "awful reputation" (Kaestle, 1993) of education research and diminished its promise.

PUBLIC AND PROFESSIONAL INTEREST IN EDUCATION RESEARCH

While federal funding for education research has waxed and (mostly) waned, the federal government has been clear and consistent in its call for scientific research into education. The Cooperative Research Act of 1954 first authorized the then Office of Education to fund education research (National Research Council, 1992). The National Institute of Education (NIE) was created in 1971 to provide "leadership in the conduct and support of scientific inquiry into education" (General Education Provisions Act, Sec. 405; cited in National Research Council, 1992). Likewise, as NIE was incorporated into the U.S. Office of Educational Research and Improvement (OERI), the quest for the scientific conduct of education research was front and center (Department of Education Organization Act, 1979; see National Research Council, 1992).

The federal government has not been alone in calling for scientific research into education. This call has been echoed in a series of reports and recommendations from the National Academies' research arm, the National Research Council (NRC). In 1958, the NRC's report, *A Proposed Organization for Research in Education,* recommended establishing a research organization for the advancement and improvement of education. A 1977 report, *Fundamental Research and the Process of Education,* called for fundamental research about educational processes. A 1986 report, *Creating a Center for Education Statistics: A Time for Action,* led to what many regard as the successful overhaul of the federal education statistical agency. And in the 1992 report, *Research and Education Reform: Roles for the Office of Educational Research and Improvement,* the NRC called for a complete overhaul of the federal research agency, criticizing its focus on "quick solutions to poorly understood problems" (National Research Council, 1992, p. viii). The report recommended creating an infrastructure that would support and foster scientific research into learning and cognitive processes underlying education, curriculum, teaching, and education reform.

What, then, warrants another NRC report on scientific research in education? First, as we argue above, the nation's commitment to improve the education of all children requires continuing efforts to improve its research capacity. Questions concerning how to do this are currently being debated as Congress considers ways to organize a federal education research agency. Indeed, H.R. 4875—the so-called "Castle bill" to reauthorize OERI—has provided us with an opportunity to revisit historic questions about the "science of education" in a modern policy context. This bill includes definitions—crafted in the political milieu—of scientific concepts to be applied to education research, reflecting yet again a skepticism about the quality of current scholarship. (We discuss these definitions briefly in Chapter 6.) Our report is specifically intended to provide an articulation of the core nature of scientific inquiry in education from the research community.

The rapid growth of the education research community in recent years has resulted in the production of many studies, articles, journal publications, books and opinion pieces associated with academics, but that are not necessarily scientific in character. Moreover, the field of education researchers is itself a diverse mix of professionals with varying levels and types of research training, and they often bring quite different orientations to their work. These multiple perspectives are in many ways indicative of the health of the enterprise, but they also render the development of a cohesive community with self-regulating norms difficult (Lagemann, 2000). In this spirit, we intend this report to provide a balanced account of scientific quality and rigor that sparks self-reflection within the research community about its roles and responsibilities for promoting scientific quality and advancing scientific understanding.

Finally, perhaps more than ever before, citizens, business leaders, politicians, and educators want credible information on which to evaluate and guide today's reform and tomorrow's education for all students. Driven by the performance goals inherent in standards-based reforms, they seek a working consensus on the challenges confronting education, on what works in what contexts and what doesn't, and on why what works does work. Simply put, they seek trustworthy, scientific evidence on which to base decisions about education.

COMMITTEE CHARGE AND APPROACH

The committee was assembled in the fall of 2000 and was asked to complete its report by the fall of 2001. The charge from the committee's sponsor, the National Educational Policy and Priorities Board of the U.S. Department of Education, was as follows:

> This study will review and synthesize recent literature on the science and practice of scientific education research and consider how to support high quality science in a federal education research agency.

To organize its deliberations, the committee translated this mandate into three framing questions:

- What are the principles of scientific quality in education research?

To address this question, the committee considered how the purposes, norms, methods, and traditions of scientific inquiry translated in the study of education. The committee also considered what scientific quality meant, both in individual research projects and in programs of research, to better understand how knowledge could be organized, synthesized, and general-ized. Furthermore, we sought to understand how scientific education research is similar to, and different from, other scientific endeavors.

In approaching this question, we recognize that existing education research has suffered from uneven quality. This statement is not very startling, because the same could be said about virtually every area of scientific research. Although it is clear that the reputation of education research is quite poor (Kaestle, 1993; Sroufe, 1997; H.R. 4875), we do not believe it is productive to attempt to catalogue "bad research." Instead, we have found it useful to focus on constructive questions: How much good research has been produced? Why isn't there more good research? How could more good research be generated? We address these kinds of questions in the report.

- How can a federal research agency promote and protect scientific quality in the education research it supports?

The committee did *not* conduct an evaluation of OERI. Rather, the committee approached the general question of the federal role from the perspective of scientific quality and rigor. We sought to identify the key design principles for a federal agency charged with fostering the scientific integrity of the research it funds and with promoting the accumulation of science-based knowledge over time. Among the issues the committee explored were how research quality is affected by internal infrastructure mechanisms, such as peer review, as well as external forces, such as political influence and fiscal support, and how the federal role can build the capacity of the field to do high-quality scientific work.

Here again, our approach is constructive and forward looking. We attempt to strike a balance between understanding the realities of the fed-eral bureaucracy and the history of an education research agency within it while avoiding the detailed prescriptions of previous and current proposals to reform the existing federal role. We hope to make a unique contribu-tion by focusing on "first principles" that form the core of scientific edu-cation research at the federal level and providing guidance about how these principles might be implemented in practice. Some of our suggestions are already in place; some are not. Some will be easy to implement; others will be more difficult. Our intent is to provide a set of principles that can serve as a guidepost for improvement over time.

- How can research-based knowledge in education accumulate?

The committee believes that rigor in individual scientific investigations and a strong federal infrastructure for supporting such work are required for research in education to generate and nurture a robust knowledge base. Thus, in addressing this question, we focused on mechanisms that support the accumulation of knowledge from science-based education research—the organization and synthesis of knowledge generated from multiple investigations. The committee considered the roles of the professional research community, the practitioner communities, and the federal government. Since we view the accumulation of scientific knowledge as the ultimate goal of research, this issue weaves throughout the report.

Assumptions

Taking our cue from much of the historical and philosophical context we describe in this chapter, we make five core assumptions in approaching our work.

First, although science is often perceived as embodying a concise, unified view of research, the history of scientific inquiry attests to the fact there is no one method or process that unambiguously defines science. The committee has therefore taken an inclusive view of "the science of education" or "the educational sciences" in its work. This broad view, however, should not be *misinterpreted* to suggest "anything goes." Indeed, the primary purpose of this report is to provide guidance for what constitutes rigorous scientific research in education. Thus, we identify a set of principles that apply to physical and social science research and to science-based education research (Chapter 3). In conjunction with a set of features that characterize education (Chapter 4), these principles help define the domain of scientific research in education, roughly delineating what is in the domain and what is not. We argue that education research, like research in the social, biological, and physical realms, faces—as a final "court of appeal"—the test of conceptual and empirical adequacy over time. An educational hypothesis or conjecture must be judged in the light of the best array of relevant qualitative or quantitative data that can be garnered. If a hypothesis is insulated from such testing, then it cannot be considered as falling within the ambit of science.

A second assumption is that many scientific studies in education and other fields will not pan out. Research is like oil exploration—there are, on average, many dry holes for every successful well. This is not because initial decisions on where to dig were necessarily misguided. Competent oil explorers, like competent scientists, presumably used the best information available to conduct their work. Dry holes are found because there is considerable uncertainty in exploration of any kind. Sometimes exploration companies gain sufficient knowledge from a series of dry holes in an area to close it down. And in many cases, failure to find wells can shed light on why apparently productive holes turned out to be dry; in other words, the process of failing to make a grand discovery can itself be very instructive. Other times they doggedly pursue an area because the science suggests there is still a reasonable chance of success. Scientific progress advances in much the same way, as we describe in Chapter 2.

Third, we assume that it is possible to describe the physical and social world scientifically so that, for example, multiple observers can agree on what they see. Consequently, we reject the postmodernist school of thought when it posits that social science research can never generate objective or trustworthy knowledge.[2] However, we simultaneously reject research that relies solely on the narrow tenets of behaviorism/positivism (see above) (National Research Council, 2001b) because we believe its view of human nature is too simplistic.

Fourth, the committee's focus on the scientific underpinnings of research in education does not reflect a simplistic notion that scientific quality alone will improve the *use* of such research in school improvement efforts. Scientific quality and rigor are necessary, but not sufficient, conditions for improving the overall value of education research. There are major issues related to, for example, how the research enterprise should be

---

[2]This description applies to an extreme epistemological perspective that questions the rationality of the scientific enterprise altogether, and instead believes that all knowledge is based on sociological factors like power, influence, and economic factors (Phillips and Burbules, 2000).

organized at the federal and local levels, how it should and can be connected to policy and practice (National Research Council, 1999d), and the nature of scientific knowledge in education (Weiss, 1999; Murnane and Nelson, 1984). Throughout this report, we treat these complementary issues with varying degrees of depth depending on their proximity to our focus on the scientific nature of the field. Indeed, over the course of our deliberations, we have become aware of several complementary efforts focused on improving education research (e.g., NRC's Strategic Education Research Partnership, RAND panels, Education Quality Institute, Interagency Education Research Initiative, and National Academy of Education-Social Science Research Council Committee on Education Research).

Finally, and critically, the committee believes that scientific research in education is a form of scholarship that can uniquely contribute to understanding and improving education, especially when integrated with other approaches to studying human endeavors. For example, historical, philosophical, and literary scholarship can and should inform important questions of purpose and direction in education. Education is influenced by human ideals, ideologies, and judgments of value, and these things need to be subjected to rigorous—scientific and otherwise—examination.

Structure of Report

The remainder of this report moves from the general to the specific. We begin by describing the commonalities shared across all scientific endeavors, including education research. We then take up some of the specifics of education research by characterizing the nature of education and of studying it scientifically; describing a sampling of trusted research designs used to address key questions; and providing guidance on how a federal education research agency could best support high quality science. A description of the specific contents of each chapter follows.

In Chapter 2 we address the global question of whether scientific inquiry in education has generated useful insights for policy and practice. We describe and analyze several lines of work, both inside and outside of education, to compare the accumulation of knowledge in education to that of other fields. In doing so, we provide "existence proofs" of the accumulation of knowledge in education and show that its progression is similar in many ways to other fields.

In Chapter 3 we provide a set of guiding principles that undergird all scientific endeavors. We argue that at its core, scientific inquiry in education is the same as in all other scientific disciplines and fields and provide examples from a range of fields to illustrate this common set of principles.

In Chapter 4 we describe how the unique set of features that characterize education shape the guiding principles of science in education research. We argue that it is this interaction between the principles of science and the features of education that makes scientific research in education specialized. We also describe some aspects of education research as a profession to further illuminate its character.

In Chapter 5, integrating our principles of science (Chapter 3) and the features of education (Chapter 4), we then take up the topic of the design of scientific education research. Recognizing that design must go hand in hand with the problem investigated, we examine education research design (and provide several examples) across three common types of research questions: What is happening? Is there a systematic effect? and How or why is it happening?

Finally, in Chapter 6 we offer a set of design principles for a federal education research agency charged with supporting the kind of scientific research in education we describe in this report. We argue that developing a strong scientific culture is the key to a successful agency and that all education stakeholders have a role to play in it.

2

Accumulation of Scientific Knowledge

The charge to the committee reflects the widespread perception that research in education has not produced the kind of cumulative knowledge garnered from other scientific endeavors. Perhaps even more unflattering, a related indictment leveled at the education research enterprise is that it does not generate knowledge that can inform education practice and policy. The prevailing view is that findings from education research studies are of low quality and are endlessly contested—the result of which is that no consensus emerges about anything.

We argue in Chapter 1 that this skepticism is not new. Most recently, these criticisms were expressed in proposed reauthorization legislation for the Office of Educational Research and Improvement (OERI) (H.R. 4875) and related congressional testimony and debate (Fuhrman, 2001); in the committee's workshop with educators, researchers, and federal staff (National Research Council, 2001d); and at the 2001 annual meeting of the American Educational Research Association (Shavelson, Feuer, and Towne, 2001). U.S. Representative Michael Castle (R-DE), in a press release reporting on the subcommittee's action on H.R. 4875 said:

> Education research is broken in our country . . . and Congress must work to make it more useful. . . . Research needs to be conducted on a more scientific basis. Educators and policy makers need objective, reliable research. . . .

Is this assessment accurate? Is there any evidence that scientific research in education accumulates to provide objective, reliable results? Does knowledge from scientific education research progress as it does in the physical, life, or social sciences? To shed light on these questions, we consider how knowledge accumulates in science and provide examples of the state of scientific knowledge in several fields. In doing so, we make two central arguments in this chapter.

First, research findings in education have progressed over time and provided important insights in policy and practice. We trace the history of three productive lines of inquiry related to education as "existence proofs" to support this assertion and to convey the promise for future investments in scientific education research. What is needed is more and better scientific research of this kind on education.

Our second and related argument is that in research across the scientific disciplines and in education, the path to scientific understanding shares several common characteristics. Its advancement is choppy, pushing the boundaries of what is known by moving forward in fits and starts as methods, theories, and empirical findings evolve. The path to scientific knowledge wanders through contested terrain as researchers, as well as the policy, practice, and citizen communities critically examine, interpret, and debate new findings and it requires substantial investments of time and money. Through examples from inside and outside education, we show that this characterization of scientific advancement is shared across the range of scientific endeavors.

We chose the examples that appear in this chapter to illustrate these core ideas. We do not suggest that these lines of inquiry have provided definitive answers to the underlying questions they have addressed over time. As we argue in Chapter 1, science is never "finished." Science provides a valuable source of knowledge for understanding and improving the world, but its conclusions always remain conjectural and subject to revision based on new inquiry and knowledge. As Thomas Henry Huxley once said: "The great tragedy of Science—the slaying of a beautiful hypothesis by an ugly fact" (cited in Cohn, 1989, p. 12).

Thus, the examples we highlight in this chapter show that sustained inquiry can significantly improve the *certainty* with which one can claim to understand something. Our descriptions necessarily convey the state of knowledge as it is understood today; to be sure, subsequent work is already under way in each area that will refine, and may overturn, current understanding. It is always difficult to assess the progress of a line of research at a given point in time; as Imre Lakatos once wrote: ". . . rationality works much slower than most people tend to think, and even then, fallibly" (1970, p. 174).

A final point of clarification is warranted. In this chapter we rely on the metaphor of "accumulating" knowledge. This imagery conveys two important notions. First, it suggests that scientific understanding coalesces, as it progresses, to make sense of systems, experiences, and phenomena. The imagery also connotes the idea that scientific inquiry builds on the work that has preceded it. The use of the word "accumulation" is not, however, intended to suggest that research proceeds along a linear path to ultimately culminate in a complete and clear picture of the focus of inquiry (e.g., education). Again, as we show through several examples, science advances understanding of various phenomena through sustained inquiry and debate among investigators in a field.

ILLUSTRATIONS OF KNOWLEDGE ACCUMULATION

In this section we provide examples of how scientific knowledge has accumulated in four areas. First, we describe the progression of scientific insight in differential gene activation, a line of inquiry in molecular biology that began 50 years ago and laid the foundation for today's groundbreaking human genome project. Next, we trace advances in understanding how to measure and assess human performance, including educational achievement, that have evolved over more than a century. We then describe two controversial but productive lines of research in education: phonological awareness and early reading skill development, and whether and how schools and resources matter to children's achievement.

These examples are provided to illustrate that lines of scientific inquiry in education research can generate cumulative knowledge with a degree of certainty and that they do so in ways similar to other scientific endeavors. To be sure, the nature of the work varies considerably across the examples. We address broad similarities and differences among disciplines and fields in Chapters 3 and 4. The lines of inquiry in this chapter demonstrate how knowledge is acquired through systematic scientific study.

Differential Gene Activation

The rise of molecular biology and the modern concept of the gene provides an especially clear illustration of the progression of scientific understanding in the life sciences. The earliest model of the gene was derived from Mendel's pea plant experiments in the 1860s. Mendel concluded that these plants exhibited dominant and recessive traits that were inherited. The key concept at this stage was the trait itself, with no attempt to conceptualize the physical mechanism by which the trait was passed on from generation to generation (Derry, 1999). By the time Mendel's work became known to the scientific world, cell biologists with newly improved microscopes had identified the threadlike structures in the nuclei of cells called chromosomes, which soon became known through experiments as the carriers of hereditary information. It was quickly recognized that some traits, eventually to be called genes, were inherited together (linked), and that the linkage was due to those genes being located on the same chromosome. Using breeding experiments with strains of various organisms, some having altered (mutated) genes, geneticists began to map various genes to their chromosomes. But there was still no conceptualization of the nature or structure of the genes themselves.

The next refinement of the model was to identify the gene as a molecular structure, which required the development of biochemical and physical techniques for working with large, complex molecules. Although other experiments at nearly the same time pointed to deoxyribonucleic acid (DNA) as carrying genetic information, the structure of DNA was not yet known. Scientists of the day were reluctant to accept the conclusion that DNA is the primary hereditary material because a molecule composed of only four base units, it was thought, could hardly store all the information about an organism's features. Moreover, there was no mechanism known for passing such information on from one generation to the next.

It was these developments that led to the watershed discovery by Watson and Crick (1953) (and related work of a host of other scientists in the emerging field of molecular biology) of the DNA double helix and the subsequent evidence that genes are lengths of DNA composed of specific sequences of its four basic elements. The double helix structure that Watson and Crick discovered from analyzing DNA X-ray diffraction data also was crucial because it suggested a major revision to the extant model of how the molecule can replicate itself.

Genetic analysis by Francois Jacob and Jacques Monod, also in the 1950s, showed that in addition to providing the templates for constructing important proteins, some genes code regulatory proteins that can turn specific sets of genes on or off (see Alberts et al., 1997). Early work on gene regulation had suggested that when the sugar lactose is present in the nutrient medium of the common bacterium E. coli, the bacteria produce a set of enzymatic proteins that are responsible for metabolizing that sugar. If the lactose is removed from the medium, those enzymes disappear. The first evidence that led to an understanding of gene regulation was the discovery that there were mutant strains of E. coli in which those enzymes never disappeared because the bacteria were unable to shut off specific sets of genes. Previous work had shown that mutations—changes in one or more nucleotides in the gene sequence—could alter the activity of enzymatic proteins by changing the protein structure. Thus, it was first hypothesized that in these mutant E. coli strains, mutations resulted in some enzymes being changed to an "always-on" state. Again, this model was later shown to be invalid when Jacob and Monod demonstrated experimentally that these mutant bacteria were instead deficient in the proteins that served as regulators that specifically repressed (or "turned off") those sets of genes.

Because most regulatory proteins are present in cells in minute quantities, it required more than a decade for advances in cell fractionation and purification to isolate these repressor proteins by chromatography. But once isolated, the proteins were shown to bind to specific DNA sequences, usually adjacent to the genes that they regulate. The order of nucleotide bases in these DNA sequences could then be determined by a combination of classical genetics and molecular sequencing techniques.

This is just the beginning of the story. This work has led to new knowledge in molecular biology that affects our understanding of both cell development and of genetic disease. The work of countless molecular biologists in the past 50 years has resulted in the recent publication of the linear "map" of the entire human genome, from which, one day—perhaps many years in the future—all genetically influenced diseases and all developmental steps may be deduced.

Now, after half a century of publications describing these fundamental discoveries, the theoretical model of the gene can be tested in DNA microarrays the size of a postage stamp that promulgate up to 60 million DNA/RNA (ribonucleic acid) reactions simultaneously (Gibbs, 2001). Over 1,100 disease-related genes have been discovered that are associated with almost 1,500 serious clinical disorders (Peltonen and McKusick, 2001). More than 1,000 mutations have been linked to cystic fibrosis alone, for example. Uncertainties that must be resolved by future research revolve around which of those genes or gene complexes are critical for the onset of the disease and how to correct for the errors.

Testing and Assessment

The recorded history of testing is over four millennia old (Du Bois, 1970); by the middle of the nineteenth century, written examinations were used in Europe and in the United States for such high-stakes purposes as awarding degrees, government posts, and licenses in law, teaching, and medicine. Today, the nation relies heavily on tests to assess students' achievement, reading comprehension, motivation, self-concept, political attitudes, career aspirations, and the like. The evolution of the science of educational testing, similar in many ways to the progress in genetics, follows a long line of work in educational psychology, psychometrics, and related fields dating back to the late 1800s. We take up the evolution of testing over the past 150 years when the *scientific* study of tests and assessments was still in its infancy. Steady but contested and nonlinear progress has been made since the early days, often from the melding of mathematics and psychology: "Criticizing test theory . . . becomes a matter of comparing what the mathematician assumes with what the psychologist can reasonably believe about people's responses" (Cronbach, 1989, p. 82).

This evolution can be seen in the development of three related strands of work in this field: reliability, validity, and mathematical modeling.

Test Reliability

The notion of test reliability—the consistency of scores produced by a test—grew out of the recognition that test scores could differ from one occasion to another even when the individual being tested had not changed. The original notion of reliability was based on the simplifying assumption that a single underlying trait accounted for widely observed consistency in test performance and that variations in test scores for the same person at different times were due to an undifferentiated, constant measurement error. While the mathematics for dealing with reliability under these assumptions was straightforward (a correlation coefficient—see below), Thorndike (1949), Guttman (1953), and Cronbach (1951, 1971), among others, recognized that the assumptions did not align with what could be reasonably believed about human behavior. For example, in practice different methods of calculating a reliability coefficient defined "true score"—the consistent part of a respondent's performance—and measurement error—the inconsistent part, somewhat differently. For instance, remembering an answer to a particular question when the same test was administered twice meant that "memory" contributed to a respondent's consistency or true score, but not so upon taking parallel forms of the test. Moreover, Cronbach, Guttman, Thorndike, and others recognized that test performance is more complex than what a single trait could predict, and that there can be many sources of measurement error including inconsistency due to different occasions, different test forms, different test administrations, and the like.

In the late 1800s, Edgeworth (1888) applied the theory of probability to model the uncertainty in the scores that graders assigned to essays. He estimated how many examinees who had failed to get college honors, would have slipped over the "honors line" had there been different, but equally competent, graders. Krueger and Spearman (1907) introduced the term "reliability coefficient." They used a measure similar to the correlation coefficient (a measure of the strength of the relationship between two variables) that extended Edgeworth's ideas and provided a measure of the difference in the rankings of individuals that would occur had the assessment consisted of different but comparable test questions. The Spearman-Brown (Spearman, 1910; Brown, 1910) formula gave researchers a way to estimate the reliability of a test of a certain length without having to give both it *and* a "comparable version" of it to the same examinees. Kelley (1923) in an early text gave a detailed treatment of various "reliability coefficients." Kuder and Richardson (1937) produced a more streamlined technique that also did not require obtaining the performance of the same individuals on two tests. However, in working with the Kuder-Richardson formulas, Cronbach (1989) found that at times it produced numbers that were not believable—e.g., sometimes the estimated reliability was negative. In response, he (Cronbach, 1951) extended this work by providing a general formula that fit a very wide class of situations, not just dichotomously scored test questions.

Once easily usable formulas were available for computing measures of a test's reliability, these measures could be used to study the factors that affect reliability. This led to improved test development and to the gradual recognition that different test uses required different measures of test reliability. In the 1960s, Cronbach, Rajaratnam, and Gleser (1963), drawing on advances in statistical theory (especially Fisher's variance partitioning and random components of variance theory) incorporated this understanding into a framework that accounted, simultaneously, for multiple sources of measurement error. Generalizability theory (Cronbach, Gleser, Nanda and Rajaratnam, 1972), now provides a systematic analysis of the many facets that affect test score consistency and measurement error.

Test Validity

In a similar manner, the concept of test validity—initially conceived as the relation between test scores and later performance—has evolved as straightforward mathematical equations have given way to a growing understanding of human behavior. At first, validity was viewed as a characteristic of the test. It was then recognized that a test might be put to multiple uses and that a given test might be valid for some uses but not for others. That is, validity came to be understood as a characteristic of the *interpretation and use* of test scores, and not of the test itself, because the very same test (e.g., reading test) could be used to predict academic performance, estimate the level of an individual's proficiency, and diagnose problems. Today, validity theory incorporates both test interpretation and use (e.g., intended and unintended social consequences).

While the problem of relating test results to later performance is quite old, Wissler (1901) was the first to make extensive use of the correlation coefficient, developed a decade earlier, to measure the strength of this relationship. He showed that the relationship between various physical and mental laboratory measures with grades in college was too small to have any practical predictive value. Spearman (1904b) discussed factors that distort measured correlation coefficients: these included ignoring variation in the ages of the children tested as well as other factors that affect both quantities being correlated and the correlation of quantities subject to substantial measurement error.

The "Army Alpha" test was developed in 1917 for use in classification and assignment during World War I. It forced the rapid development of group testing and with it the increased need for test validation that was interpreted primarily as the correlation of the test with other "outside" criteria. Gulliksen's (1950a) work during World War II with tests used by the Navy to select engineers led him to emphasize a test's "intrinsic content validity" as well as its correlations with other criteria in test validation studies. By 1954, the American Psychological Association recognized three forms of test validity—content, criterion-related, and construct validity.

In 1971, Cronbach put forth, and in 1993 Messick reaffirmed, the current view that validity is a property of the uses and inferences made on the basis of test scores rather than a property of a test. In this view, the establishment of the validity of an inference is a complex process that uses a variety of systematic evidence from many sources including test content, correlations with other quantities, and the consequences of the intended use of the test scores. Because of the variety of test uses and of the evidence that can be brought to bear on the validity of each use, claims for and against test validity are potentially the most contested aspects of testing in both the scientific and public policy arenas.

Mathematical Models

The mathematical models and theories underlying the analysis of tests have also evolved from modest beginnings. These models were first introduced in the beginning of the twentieth century as single-factor models to explain correlations among mental ability tests. Spearman (1904a) introduced his "one factor" model to explain the positive intercorrelations between various tests of mental abilities. (This led directly to his original definition of test reliability.) This unidimensional view of general ability (intelligence) or "g" immediately raised controversy about the nature of human abilities. Thurstone (1931), assuming a multidimensional structure of intelligence developed more complicated multifactor analysis models and Guilford (1967) posited no less than 120 factors based on three fundamental dimensions. In perhaps the most comprehensive analysis to date, Carroll (1993; see also Gustafsson and Undheim, 1996) found strong empirical support for a hierarchical model.

These mathematical models then evolved to classical reliability theory with a single underlying trait. The mathematical models developed in close conjunction with the increasingly more complicated uses of tests and more complex demands made on the inferences based on them.

Kelley (1923) gave an exposition of "true score theory" that provides precise definitions to various different quantities, all called "test reliability," and introduced his formula relating observed scores, true scores, and test reliability. This led to classical test theory, which was codified in Gulliksen (1950b). However, this theory was limited in its simple, unidimensional conception of behavior and its undifferentiated notion of measurement error (noted above). Moreover, as Lord (1952) pointed out, this test theory ignored information about the nature of the test items (e.g., difficulty) that individuals were responding to. With the advent of high speed computing, the integration of the trait focus of test theory with information about test-item characteristics led to a major advance in scaling test scores—item-response theory.

Item response theory (IRT) (Lord, 1952), a detailed mathematical model of test performance at the test question level, developed over the next few decades, with major publications by Rasch (1960) and Lord and Novick (1968). IRT expanded quickly and is now a very active area of research. There are several important applications of IRT: development of item and test information curves for use in test development; detailed analyses of item-level data; pooling data from related assessments given to different examinees; linking scores on different tests; reporting scores on a common scale for tests—such as the National Assessment of Educational Progress—for which each examinee only takes a small portion of the whole assessment; and the creation of "adaptive tests" given on computers.

Current developments include using IRT to model the cognitive and evidentiary reasoning processes involved in answering test questions so as to improve the use of tests in diagnosis and learning (National Research

Council, 2001b). The next evolution of models most likely will incorporate what are called "Bayesian inference nets" to construct appropriate theory-driven interpretations of complex test performance (Mislevy, 1996; National Research Council, 2001b).

Phonological Awareness and Early Reading Skills

A third example traces the history of inquiry into the role of phonological awareness, alphabetic knowledge, and other beginning reading skills. This research has generated converging evidence that phonological awareness is a necessary, but not sufficient, competency for understanding the meaning embedded in print, which is the ultimate goal of learning to read.

Research on the role of phonological awareness and alphabetic knowledge in beginning reading began at the Haskins Laboratories in the 1960s under the leadership of Isabelle Liberman, a psychologist and educator, and her husband, Alvin Liberman, a speech scientist. At the time, Alvin Liberman and his colleagues were interested in constructing a reading machine for the blind. They made important observations about the production and perception of speech that they hypothesized might be related to the development of reading. Most pertinent was the observation that speech is segmented phonologically, although the user of speech may not consciously recognize this segmented nature because phonological segments are merged together during speech production (A.L. Liberman, Cooper, Shankweiler, and Studdert-Kennedy, 1967). So a word like "bag," which actually has three segments represented at a phonemic level, is heard as one sound as phonological segments are merged together in speech.

Isabelle Liberman subsequently applied these observations to reading, hypothesizing that the phonetic segments of speech that are more or less represented in print might not be readily apparent to a young child learning to read (I. Liberman, 1971). It had long been recognized that teaching the relationship of sounds and letters helped children develop word recognition capacities (Chall, 1967). What was unique about the Haskins research was the clear recognition that written language is scaffolded, or built, on oral language and that literacy is a product of long-established human capabilities for speech (A.M. Liberman, 1997). But speech is usually learned naturally without explicit instruction. In order to learn to read (and write), the relationship of speech and print (i.e., the alphabetic principle) typically must be taught since children do not naturally recognize the relationship. This principle helps explain the role of phonics—instructional practices that emphasize how spellings are related to speech sounds—in beginning reading instruction.

In a series of studies, the Libermans and their colleagues systematically evaluated these hypotheses. They demonstrated that young children were not aware of the segmented nature of speech, that this awareness developed over time, and that its development was closely linked with the development of word recognition skills (Shankweiler, 1991). They emphasized that phonological awareness is an oral language skill and is not the same as phonics. However, the research demonstrated that these capabilities are necessary, though not sufficient, for learning to read (Blachman, 2000); proficient reading comprehension requires additional linguistic and cognitive capabilities. Thus, it was necessary to integrate research on word recognition with the broader field of reading research. Children vary considerably in how easily they develop phonological awareness and grasp the alphabetic principle, which has led to controversy about how explicitly it should be taught (Stanovich, 1991; 2000).

From these origins in the 1960s and early 1970s, research on phonological awareness and reading expanded (Stanovich, 1991; 2000). In the latter part of the 1970s, struggling against a background of older theories that were behavioristic or focused on the role of perceptual factors in reading (e.g., Gibson and Levin, 1975), the view of written language as scaffolded on oral language gradually took hold—despite criticisms that the research was simplistic and reductionistic (e.g., Satz and Fletcher, 1980). In the 1980s, research expanded into areas that involved the development of phonological awareness and reading capabilities, ultimately leading to large-scale longitudinal studies showing that phonological awareness could be measured reliably in young children and that its development preceded the onset of word recognition skills (Wagner, Torgesen, and Rashotte, 1994). Other research strengthened findings concerning the critical relationship of phonological awareness skills and word recognition deficits in children, adolescents, and adults who had reading difficulties. This led directly to reconceptualizations of disorders such as dyslexia as word-level reading disabilities caused by problems developing phonological awareness and the ensuing development of another program of research to evaluate this hypothesis (Vellutino, 1979; Shaywitz, 1996).

These later findings were of great interest to people studying learning disabilities, who expressed concern about whether the findings were being applied to children in the classroom and whether they were being used to understand reading failure. In 1985, at the request of Congress, the National Institute of Child Health and Human Development (NICHD) was asked to initiate a research program on learning disabilities. This program led to research on multiple factors underlying reading disability, including research on cognitive factors, the brain, genetics, and instruction.[1] Many studies varying in research questions and methods have built on and emerged from these initiatives. For example, epidemiological studies of the prevalence of reading disabilities in North America, the United Kingdom, and New Zealand showed that reading skills were normally distributed in the population. This finding was a major breakthrough because it meant that children who were poor readers were essentially in the lower part of the continuum of all readers, rather than qualitatively different from good readers (Shaywitz et al., 1992). These studies overturned prevailing notions about reading disability that reported non-normality and implied qualitative differences between good and poor readers that had led to theories specific to the poor reader; rather, these findings indicated that the same theory could be used to explain good and poor reading. The prevalence studies also showed that most poor readers had word recognition difficulties and that the prevalence of reading failure was shockingly high (Fletcher and Lyon, 1998).

These studies were pivotal for other areas of inquiry, and convergence has slowly emerged across different domains of inquiry: cognitive, genetic, brain, and ultimately, instruction. Cognitive studies explored the limits of phonological processing and word recognition in poor readers using a

---

[1]Several other federal agencies (e.g., the U.S. Department of Education Office of Special Education Programs, the Head Start Bureau, the former National Institute of Education) and research in other countries contributed substantially to this knowledge base. To give a sense of the scope of the effort, the research at NICHD alone involves scientists at 44 sites and the study of more than 42,500 children and adults, some for as long as 18 years. NICHD's total expenditures since 1965—again, only at a single agency involved in a broader effort across federal agencies—exceeds $100 million.

variety of models stemming from laboratory-based research on reading. Many methods and paradigms were used: developmental studies, information processing studies focusing on connectionistic models of the reading process, eye movement studies, psychometric studies oriented to measurement, and observational studies of teachers in classrooms—a broad approach. Genetic studies (Olson, Forsberg, Gayan and DeFries, 1999; Pennington, 1999; Olson, 1999; Grigorenko, 1999) showed that reading skills were heritable, but that heritability only accounted for 50 percent of the variability in reading skills: the remainder reflects environmental factors, including instruction. Functional brain imaging studies—possible only over the past few years—have identified neural networks that support phonological processing and word recognition. These findings have been replicated in several laboratories using different neuroimaging methods and reflect more than 20 years of research to identify reliable neural correlates of reading disability (Eden and Zeffiro, 1998).

Current and future work in reading skill development is sure to build on and refine this base. Indeed, under the leadership of several federal agencies—NICHD, Department of Education, and National Science Foundation (NSF)—instruction research has now come to the forefront of how to "scale up" education research for reading (as well as mathematics and science) for pre-kindergarten through high school (preK-12). This intervention and implementation research itself has a long history and is closely linked with other lines of inquiry. The research takes place in schools, which need to be seen as complex social organizations embedded in a larger context of communities, universities, and government. However, the origins are still in basic research, still connected with the "big idea" of the 1960s and the accumulation of knowledge since then.

This line of research evolved over 30 years, and accelerated, albeit along a jagged and contested course, when significant federal leadership and funding became available. The National Research Council (1998) and the National Reading Panel (2000), as well as Adams (1990) have summarized this body of research.

Education Resources and Student Achievement

Perhaps the most contentious area in current education research is the role of schools and resources in education outcomes. For much of the twentieth century, most policy makers and members of the public believed that increases in education resources (e.g., money, curricula, and facilities) led to improved education outcomes, such as student achievement (Cohen, Raudenbush, and Ball, in press).[2] However, over the past few decades, research has shown that these direct relationships between resources and outcomes are either very weak or elusive—perhaps products of wishful or somewhat simplistic thinking.

Beginning with Coleman et al.'s (1966) *Equality of Educational Opportunity* (see also Jencks et al., 1972), social science research began to document the relative absence of direct schooling effects on student achievement in comparison with the effects of students' background characteristics. It became clear that resources such as money, libraries, and curricula had, at best, a very weak effect on students' achievement, a counterintuitive finding. Rather, students' home background (parents' educational and social backgrounds) had the biggest effect on their achievement.

Needless to say, the Coleman finding was controversial because it seemed to say that schools don't make a difference in student learning. This is not exactly what Coleman and others had found (see Coleman, Hoffer, and Kilgore, 1982), but rather how it has been (mis)interpreted over time. The key finding was that school-to-school differences were not nearly as large relative to student-to-student differences as had been supposed. Moreover, most economic studies of the *direct* relationship between educational resources (especially money) and student outcomes have reached conclusions similar to Coleman et al. (1966) and Jencks et al. (1972) (see, especially, Hanushek, 1981, 1986, Hedges, Laine and Greenwald, 1994; Loeb and Page, 2000; Mosteller, 1995). As Cohen et al. (in press) explained, this was "an idea which many conservatives embraced to support arguments against liberal social policy, and which liberals rejected in an effort to retain such policies" (p. 3).

Coleman's work spawned a great deal of research attempting to find out if "schools do matter." An argument was made that Coleman's notion of how schools worked (e.g., resources represented as library holdings) was too simple (e.g., Rutter, Maughan, Mortimore, Ousten, and Smith, 1979). That is, Coleman had not adequately captured either how school and class-

---

[2]We draw heavily on this article in this section.

room processes *transform* educational resources such as money into education outcomes or how contextual factors (e.g., local job markets in competition for college graduates) affect the direct effects of (say) teachers' pay on student outcomes (Loeb and Page, 2000).

Cohen et al. (in press) traced several lines of inquiry that have, over time, begun to establish links between resources, transformational educational processes, and student outcomes. One line of work begun in the 1970s and 1980s compared more and less effective teachers as measured by students' gains in achievement. Brophy and Good (1986) found—perhaps not surprisingly—that in contrast to less effective teachers, unusually effective teachers were more likely to have "planned lessons carefully, selected appropriate materials, made their goals clear to students, maintained a brisk pace in lessons, checked student work regularly, and taught material again when students had trouble learning" (Cohen et al., in press, p.4). Another line of inquiry examined teacher-student interactions around specific content learning. These studies found that overall, time on task (time being the resource) was unrelated to students' achievement. "Only when the nature of academic tasks was taken into account were effects on learning observed" (Cohen et al., in press, p. 5; see also Palinscar and Brown, 1984; Brown, 1992). Still another line of inquiry focused on school processes, attempting to find what made the difference between more and less effective schools (e.g., Edmonds, 1984; Stedman, 1985). The more effective schools could be distinguished from their less effective counterparts by how they translated resources into education practices. High-performing schools had faculty and staff who shared a vision of instructional purpose, who believed that all students could learn, who believed that they were responsible for helping students learn, and who committed themselves to improving students' academic performance.

This line of teaching and schooling research, continuing today, has provided evidence that the "theory" of direct effects of educational resources on student outcomes (e.g., achievement) may be too simple. Suppose, following Cohen et al. (in press) that resources were viewed as a necessary but not sufficient condition for productive education, and educational experiences were viewed as the mechanism through which resources are transformed into student outcomes. It may be that resources do matter when translated into productive learning experiences for students. Some policy research now is opening up the "black box" of education production and examining just how resources are used to create educational learning experiences that may lead, in turn, to improved student achievement. This focus on educational experiences as a medium through which resources get translated is leading to (microlevel) work on classroom instruction.

A very different line of (macrolevel) work is focused on incentives and organizational structures of schools. This work is premised on the notion that adequately describing the complexity of classrooms and of alternative ways of stimulating student learning is beyond the current capacity of research methods. Therefore, an alternative approach is concentrating research efforts on understanding how different incentive structures affect student outcomes (Hanushek et al., 1994).

Both of these avenues of research build on existing evidence. Their divergent foci, however, illustrate how sophisticated scientific inquiry, addressing the same basic questions, can legitimately pursue different directions when the underlying phenomena are not well understood.

CONDITIONS FOR AND CHARACTERISTICS OF SCIENTIFIC KNOWLEDGE ACCUMULATION

This walk though the history of several lines of inquiry in educational research, alongside the stories of how knowledge has been integrated and synthesized in other areas, serves to highlight common conditions for, and characteristics of, the accumulation of knowledge in science-based research. The examples also show that educational research, like other sciences, often involves technical and theoretical matters of some complexity.

Enabling Conditions

Certain enabling conditions must be in place for scientific knowledge to grow. The clearest condition among them is time. In each of the diverse examples we provided—in molecular biology, psychological testing, early reading skills, and school resources—the accumulation of knowledge has taken decades, and in some cases centuries, to evolve to its current state. And while we chose these examples to highlight productive lines of inquiry, the findings that we highlight in this report may be revised or even proven wrong 50 years from now.

A second condition for knowledge accumulation is fiscal support. As our example of the role of phonological awareness and early reading proficiencies in particular suggests, building the education research knowledge base and moving towards scientific consensus may take significant federal leadership and investment. The many compelling reasons for increased federal leadership and investment will be explored more fully in Chapter 6.

A final condition that facilitates this accumulation is public support for sustained scientific study. For example, the public posture toward medical research, including the mapping of the human genome and related molecular study, is fundamentally different than it is toward education research. Citizens and their elected leaders acknowledge that investing in medical science is needed, and the funding pattern of federal agencies reflects this attitude (National Research Council, 2001c). Although difficult to measure precisely, it seems clear that by and large, the public trusts scientists to develop useful knowledge about foundations of disease and their prevention and treatment. In contrast, in education research technical achievements are often ignored, and research findings tend to be dismissed as irrelevant or (sometimes vehemently) discredited through public advocacy campaigns when they do not comport with conventional wisdom or ideological views. Further, with dispute about scientific quality, findings from poorly conducted studies are often used to contradict the conclusions of higher quality studies. In the social realm, people and policy makers do not tend to distinguish between scientific and political debate as they do in medical and other "hard" sciences, seriously weakening the case for such research- and evidence-based decision making. The difficulties associated with conducting randomized experiments in education is particularly problematic (Cook, 2001; Burtless, in press). The early reading example we provide is an exception in this regard: the significant and sustained congressional support beginning in the 1980s was a crucial factor in the progress of this line of work.

Common Characteristics

The nature of the progression of scientific insight across these examples also exhibits common characteristics. In all cases, the accumulation of knowledge was accomplished through fits and starts—that is, it did not move directly from naïveté to insight. Rather, the path to scientific understanding wandered over time, buffeted by research findings, methodological advances, new ideas or theories, and the political and ideological ramifications of the results. As scientists follow new paths, blind alleys are not uncommon; indeed, trying things out in the face of uncertainty is a natural and fundamental part of the scientific process (Schum, 1994; National Research Council, 2001d). Nevertheless, scientific research has a "hidden hand" (Lindblom and Cohen, 1979) that seems to lead to self-correction as debates and resolutions occur and new methods, empirical findings, or theories emerge to shed light on and change fundamental perceptions about an issue (e.g., Shavelson, 1988; Weiss, 1980).

A second characteristic of knowledge accumulation is that it is contested. Scientists are trained and employed to be skeptical observers, to ask critical questions, and to challenge knowledge claims in constructive dialogue with their peers. Indeed, we argue in subsequent chapters that it is essentially these norms of the scientific community engaging in such professional critique of each other's work that enables scientific consensus and extends the boundaries of what is known. As analytic methods for synthesizing knowledge across several studies (e.g., meta-analysis) have advanced rapidly in recent decades (Cooper and Hedges, 1994), they have enhanced the ability to make summary statements about the state-of-the-art knowledge in particular areas. These techniques are particularly useful in fields like education in which findings tend to contradict one another across studies, and thus are an increasingly important tool for discovering, testing, and explaining the diversity of these findings. The Cochrane Collaboration in medical research and the new Campbell Collaboration in social, behavioral, and educational arenas (see Box 2-1) use such methods to develop reviews that synthesize findings across studies.

In each example, the substantial progress we feature does not imply that the research community is of one mind. In all fields, scientists debate the merits of scientific findings as they attempt to integrate individual findings with existing knowledge. In education and related social sciences, this debate is intensified because of the range of legitimate disciplinary perspectives that bear on it (see Chapter 4). This issue is aptly characterized by the proverbial description of an elephant being studied by seven blind scientists, each touching a different part of the animal. Indeed, the social sciences have been characterized by increasing specialization of method and theory, with each method–theory pair describing a different aspect of a social phenomenon (Smelser, 2001).

Another source of controversy among scientists arises out of differing views about what is possible in policy and practice. For example, some policy studies (e.g., Hanushek, 1986, 1997; also see Burtless, 1996) conclude that the *indirect* effects of resources on student outcomes are both small and, as policy instruments, difficult to manage. For them, establishing the direct effect of a resource—such as selecting teachers for their subject and cognitive ability—is a more manageable policy instrument that is more likely to affect student achievement than, say, difficult-to-control indirect mechanisms such as teaching practices.

The examples in this chapter demonstrate a third characteristic of scientific knowledge generation and accumulation: the interdependent and cyclic nature of empirical findings, methodological developments, and theory building. Theory and method build on one another both as a contributor to and a consequence of empirical observations and assertions about knowledge. New knowledge gained from increased precision in measurement (say) increases the accuracy of theory. An increasingly accurate theory suggests the possibility of new measurement techniques. Application of these new measurement techniques, in turn, produces new empirical evidence, and so the cycle continues. This cycle is characteristic of the natural sciences, as illustrated in our example of differential gene activation, and also evident in social science in the measurement of economic and social indicators (deNeufville, 1975; Sheldon, 1975) and education measurement (National Research Council, 2001b).

A fourth and final characteristic that emerges from these examples is a comparative one: studying humans is inherently complex. Humans are complex beings, and modeling their behavior, belief systems, actions, character traits, location in culture, and volition is intrinsically complicated. Research challenges arise in large part because social scientists lack the high degree of control over their subjects that is typical in the "hard" sciences—for example, gaggles of molecules are better behaved than a classroom of third-graders. This observation is not intended to suggest that science is incompatible with the study of the human world. Nor do we mean to say that scientific work is fundamentally different in these domains (indeed, the main message of Chapter 3 is that the core principles of science apply across all fields). Rather, scientific inquiry involving humans is qualitatively more complex than inquiry in the natural sciences, and thus scientific understanding often requires an integration of knowledge across a rich array of paradigms, schools of thought, and approaches (Smelser, 2001).

CONCLUDING COMMENT

Science is an important source of knowledge for addressing social problems, but it does not stand in isolation. If we had continued our story about school resources and entered the current debate around education reform, we could readily show that the generation of scientific knowledge—particularly in social realms—does not guarantee its public adoption. Rather, scientific findings interact with differing views in practical and political arenas (Lindblom and Wodehouse, 1993; Feldman and March, 1981; Weiss, 1998b, 1999; Bane, 2001; Reimers and McGinn, 1997). The scientist discovers the basis for what is possible. The practitioner, parent, or policy maker, in turn, has to consider what is practical, affordable, desirable, and credible. While we argue that a failure to differentiate between scientific and political debate has hindered scientific progress and use, scientific work in the social realm—to a much greater extent than in physics or biology—will always take place in the context of, and be influenced by, social trends, beliefs, and norms.

Finally, we acknowledge that the degree to which knowledge has accumulated in the physical and life sciences exceeds that accumulation in the social sciences (e.g., Smelser, 2001) and far exceeds it in education. And there is clearly very hard work to be done to bring the kind of science-based research we highlight in this chapter to bear on education practice and policy. Indeed, scholars have long recognized that some aspects of human knowledge are not easily articulated (Polanyi, 1958). Some have argued that knowledge in education in particular is often tacit and less precise than other fields (Murnane and Nelson, 1984), rendering its use in practice more difficult than for other fields (Nelson, 2000). But, above all, the examples we provide in this chapter suggest what is possible; the goal should be to build on their successes to forge additional ones.

3

Guiding Principles for Scientific Inquiry

I n Chapter 2 we present evidence that scientific research in education accumulates just as it does in the physical, life, and social sciences. Consequently, we believe that such research would be worthwhile to pursue to build further knowledge about education, and about education policy and practice. Up to this point, however, we have not addressed the questions "What constitutes scientific research?" and "Is scientific research on education different from scientific research in the social, life, and physical sciences?" We do so in this chapter.

These are daunting questions that philosophers, historians, and scientists have debated for several centuries (see Newton-Smith [2000] for a current assessment). Merton (1973), for example, saw commonality among the sciences. He described science as having four aims: universalism, the quest for general laws; organization, the quest to organize and conceptualize a set of related facts or observations; skepticism, the norm of questioning and looking for counter explanations; and communalism, the quest to develop a community that shares a set of norms or principles for doing science. In contrast, some early modern philosophers (the logical positivists) attempted to achieve unity across the sciences by reducing them all to physics, a program that ran into insuperable technical difficulties (Trant, 1991).

In short, we hold that there are both commonalities and differences across the sciences. At a general level, the sciences share a great deal in common, a set of what might be called epistemological or fundamental principles that guide the scientific enterprise. They include seeking conceptual (theoretical) understanding, posing empirically testable and refutable hypotheses, designing studies that test and can rule out competing counterhypotheses, using observational methods linked to theory that enable other scientists to verify their accuracy, and recognizing the importance of both independent replication and generalization. It is very unlikely that any one study would possess all of these qualities. Nevertheless, what unites scientific inquiry is the primacy of empirical test of conjectures and formal hypotheses using well-codified observation methods and rigorous designs, and subjecting findings to peer review. It is, in John Dewey's expression, "competent inquiry" that produces what philosophers call "knowledge claims" that are justified or "warranted" by pertinent, empirical evidence (or in mathematics, deductive proof). Scientific reasoning takes place amid (often quantifiable) uncertainty (Schum, 1994); its assertions are subject to challenge, replication, and revision as knowledge is refined over time. The long-term goal of much of science is to produce theory that can offer a stable encapsulation of "facts" that generalizes beyond the particular. In this chapter, then, we spell out what we see as the commonalities among all scientific endeavors.

As our work began, we attempted to distinguish scientific investigations in education from those in the social, physical, and life sciences by exploring the philosophy of science and social science; the conduct of physical, life, and social science investigations; and the conduct of scientific research on education. We also asked a panel of senior government officials who fund and manage research in education and the social and behavioral sciences, and a panel of distinguished scholars from psychometrics, linguistic anthropology, labor economics and law, to distinguish principles of evidence across fields (see National Research Council, 2001d). Ultimately, we failed to convince ourselves that at a fundamental level beyond the differences in specialized techniques and objects of inquiry across the individual sciences, a meaningful distinction could be made among social, physical, and life science research and scientific research in education. At times we thought we had an example that would demonstrate the distinction, only to find our hypothesis refuted by evidence that the distinction was not real.

Thus, the committee concluded that the set of guiding principles that apply to scientific inquiry in education are the same set of principles that can be found across the full range of scientific inquiry. Throughout this chapter we provide examples from a variety of domains—in political science, geophysics, and education—to demonstrate this shared nature. Although there is no universally accepted description of the elements of scientific inquiry, we have found it convenient to describe the scientific process in terms of six interrelated, but not necessarily ordered,[1] principles of inquiry:

- Pose significant questions that can be investigated empirically.
- Link research to relevant theory.
- Use methods that permit direct investigation of the question.
- Provide a coherent and explicit chain of reasoning.
- Replicate and generalize across studies.
- Disclose research to encourage professional scrutiny and critique.

We choose the phrase "guiding principles" deliberately to emphasize the vital point that they guide, but do not provide an algorithm for, scientific inquiry. Rather, the guiding principles for scientific investigations provide a framework indicating how inferences are, in general, to be supported (or refuted) by a core of interdependent processes, tools, and practices. Although any single scientific study may not fulfill all the principles—for example, an initial study in a line of inquiry will not have been replicated independently—a strong line of research is likely to do so (e.g., see Chapter 2).

We also view the guiding principles as constituting a code of conduct that includes notions of ethical behavior. In a sense, guiding principles operate like norms in a community, in this case a community of scientists; they are expectations for how scientific research will be conducted. Ideally, individual scientists internalize these norms, and the community monitors them. According to our analysis these principles of science are common to systematic study in such disciplines as astrophysics, political science, and economics, as well as to more applied fields such as medicine, agriculture, and education. The principles emphasize objectivity, rigorous thinking, open-mindedness, and honest and thorough reporting. Numerous scholars

---

[1]For example, inductive, deductive, and abductive modes of scientific inquiry meet these principles in different sequences.

have commented on the common scientific "conceptual culture" that pervades most fields (see, e.g., Ziman, 2000, p. 145; Chubin and Hackett, 1990).

These principles cut across two dimensions of the scientific enterprise: the creativity, expertise, communal values, and good judgment of the people who "do" science; and generalized guiding principles for scientific inquiry. The remainder of this chapter lays out the communal values of the scientific community and the guiding principles of the process that enable well-grounded scientific investigations to flourish.

THE SCIENTIFIC COMMUNITY

Science is a communal "form of life" (to use the expression of the philosopher Ludwig Wittgenstein [1968]), and the norms of the community take time to learn. Skilled investigators usually learn to conduct rigorous scientific investigations only after acquiring the values of the scientific community, gaining expertise in several related subfields, and mastering diverse investigative techniques through years of practice.

The culture of science fosters objectivity through enforcement of the rules of its "form of life"—such as the need for replicability, the unfettered flow of constructive critique, the desirability of blind refereeing—as well as through concerted efforts to train new scientists in certain habits of mind. By habits of mind, we mean things such as a dedication to the primacy of evidence, to minimizing and accounting for biases that might affect the research process, and to disciplined, creative, and open-minded thinking. These habits, together with the watchfulness of the community as a whole, result in a cadre of investigators who can engage differing perspectives and explanations in their work and consider alternative paradigms. Perhaps above all, the communally enforced norms ensure as much as is humanly possible that individual scientists—while not necessarily happy about being proven wrong—are willing to open their work to criticism, assessment, and potential revision.

Another crucial norm of the scientific "form of life," which also depends for its efficacy on communal enforcement, is that scientists should be ethical and honest. This assertion may seem trite, even naïve. But scientific knowledge is constructed by the work of individuals, and like any other enterprise, if the people conducting the work are not open and candid, it can easily falter. Sir Cyril Burt, a distinguished psychologist studying the heritability of intelligence, provides a case in point. He believed so strongly in his hypothesis that intelligence was highly heritable that he "doctored" data from twin studies to support his hypothesis (Tucker, 1994; Mackintosh, 1995); the scientific community reacted with horror when this transgression came to light. Examples of such unethical conduct in such fields as medical research are also well documented (see, e.g., Lock and Wells, 1996).

A different set of ethical issues also arises in the sciences that involve research with animals and humans. The involvement of living beings in the research process inevitably raises difficult ethical questions about a host of potential risks, ranging from confidentiality and privacy concerns to injury and death. Scientists must weigh the relative benefits of what might be learned against the potential risks to human research participants as they strive toward rigorous inquiry. (We consider this issue more fully in Chapters 4 and 6.)

GUIDING PRINCIPLES

Throughout this report we argue that science is competent inquiry that produces warranted assertions (Dewey, 1938), and ultimately develops theory that is supported by pertinent evidence. The guiding principles that follow provide a framework for how valid inferences are supported, characterize the grounds on which scientists criticize one another's work, and with hindsight, describe what scientists do. Science is a creative enterprise, but it is disciplined by communal norms and accepted practices for appraising conclusions and how they were reached. These principles have evolved over time from lessons learned by generations of scientists and scholars of science who have continually refined their theories and methods.

SCIENTIFIC PRINCIPLE 1
Pose Significant Questions That Can Be Investigated Empirically

This principle has two parts. The first part concerns the nature of the questions posed: science proceeds by posing significant questions about the world with potentially multiple answers that lead to hypotheses or conjectures that can be tested and refuted. The second part concerns how these questions are posed: they must be posed in such a way that it is possible to test the adequacy of alternative answers through carefully de-signed and implemented observations.

Question Significance

A crucial but typically undervalued aspect of successful scientific in-vestigation is the quality of the question posed. Moving from hunch to conceptualization and specification of a worthwhile question is essential to scientific research. Indeed, many scientists owe their renown less to their ability to solve problems than to their capacity to select insightful questions for investigation, a capacity that is both creative and disciplined:

> The formulation of a problem is often more essential than its solu-tion, which may be merely a matter of mathematical or experi-mental skill. To raise new questions, new possibilities, to regard old questions from a new angle, requires creative imagination and marks real advance in science (Einstein and Infeld, 1938, p. 92, quoted in Krathwohl, 1998).

Questions are posed in an effort to fill a gap in existing knowledge or to seek new knowledge, to pursue the identification of the cause or causes of some phenomena, to describe phenomena, to solve a practical problem, or to formally test a hypothesis. A good question may reframe an older problem in light of newly available tools or techniques, methodological or theoretical. For example, political scientist Robert Putnam challenged the accepted wisdom that increased modernity led to decreased civic involve-ment (see Box 3-1) and his work has been challenged in turn. A question may also be a retesting of a hypothesis under new conditions or circum-stances; indeed, studies that replicate earlier work are key to robust research findings that hold across settings and objects of inquiry (see Principle 5). A good question can lead to a strong test of a theory, however explicit or implicit the theory may be.

The significance of a question can be established with reference to prior research and relevant theory, as well as to its relationship with impor-tant claims pertaining to policy or practice. In this way, scientific knowl-edge grows as new work is added to—and integrated with—the body of material that has come before it. This body of knowledge includes theo-

Does Modernization Signal the Demise of the Civic Community?

In 1970 political scientist Robert Putnam was in Rome studying Italian politics when the government decided to implement a new system of regional governments throughout the country. This situation gave Putnam and his colleagues an opportunity to begin a long-term study of how government institutions develop in diverse social environments and what affects their success or failure as democratic institutions (Putnam, Leonardi, and Nanetti, 1993). Based on a conceptual framework about "institutional performance," Putnam and his colleagues carried out three or four waves of personal interviews with government officials and local leaders, six nationwide surveys, statistical measures of institutional performance, analysis of relevant legislation from 1970 to 1984, a one-time experiment in government responsiveness, and in-depth case studies in six regions from 1976 to 1989.

The researchers found converging evidence of striking differences by region that had deep historical roots. The results also cast doubt on the then-prevalent view that increased modernity leads to decreased civic involvement. "The least civic areas of Italy are precisely the traditional southern villages. The civic ethos of traditional communities must not be idealized. Life in much of traditional Italy today is marked by hierarchy and exploitation, not by share-and-share alike" (p. 114). In contrast, "The most civic regions of Italy—the communities where citizens feel empowered to engage in collective deliberation about public choices and where those choices are translated most fully into effective public policies—include some of the most modern towns and cities of the peninsula. Modernization does not signal the demise of the civic community" (p. 115).

The findings of Putnam and his colleagues about the relative influence of economic development and civic traditions on democratic success are less conclusive, but the weight of the evidence favors the assertion that civic tradition matters more than economic affluence. This and subsequent work on social capital (Putnam, 1995) has led to a flurry of investigations and controversy that continues today.

ries, models, research methods (e.g., designs, measurements), and research tools (e.g., microscopes, questionnaires). Indeed, science is not only an effort to produce representations (models) of real-world phenomena by going from nature to abstract signs. Embedded in their practice, scientists also engage in the development of objects (e.g., instruments or practices); thus, scientific knowledge is a by-product of both technological activities and analytical activities (Roth, 2001). A review of theories and prior research relevant to a particular question can simply establish that it has not been answered before. Once this is established, the review can help shape alternative answers, the design and execution of a study by illuminating if and how the question and related conjectures have already been examined, as well as by identifying what is known about sampling, setting, and other important context.[2]

Donald Stokes' work (Stokes, 1997) provides a useful framework for thinking about important questions that can advance scientific knowledge and method (see Figure 3-1). In *Pasteur's Quadrant*, he provided evidence that the conception of research-based knowledge as moving in a linear progression from fundamental science to applied science does not reflect how science has historically advanced. He provided several examples demonstrating that, instead, many advancements in science occurred as a result of "use-inspired research," which simultaneously draws on both basic and applied research. Stokes (1997, p. 63) cites Brooks (1967) on basic and applied work:

> Work directed toward applied goals can be highly fundamental in character in that it has an important impact on the conceptual structure or outlook of a field. Moreover, the fact that research is of such a nature that it can be applied does not mean that it is not also basic.

---

[2]We recognize that important scientific discoveries are sometimes made when a competent observer notes a strange or interesting phenomenon for the first time. In these cases, of course, no prior literature exists to shape the investigation. And new fields and disciplines need to start somewhere. Our emphasis on linking to prior literature in this principle, then, applies generally to relatively established domains and fields.

Research is inspired by:

Considerations of Use?

		No	Yes
Quest for Fundamental Understanding?	Yes	Pure basic research (Bohr)	Use-inspired basic research (Pasteur)
	No		Pure applied research (Edison)

FIGURE 3-1. Quadrant model of scientific research.
SOURCE: Stokes (1997, p. 73). Reprinted with permission.

Stokes' model clearly applies to research in education, where problems of practice and policy provide a rich source for important—and often highly fundamental in character—research questions.

Empirically Based

Put simply, the term "empirical" means based on experience through the senses, which in turn is covered by the generic term observation. Since science is concerned with making sense of the world, its work is necessarily grounded in observations that can be made about it. Thus, research questions must be posed in ways that potentially allow for empirical investigation.[3] For example, both Milankovitch and Muller could collect data on the Earth's orbit to attempt to explain the periodicity in ice ages (see Box 3-2). Likewise, Putnam could collect data from natural variations in regional government to address the question of whether modernization leads to the demise of civic community (Box 3-1), and the Tennessee state legislature could empirically assess whether reducing class size improves students' achievement in early grades (Box 3-3) because achievement data could be collected on students in classes of varying sizes. In contrast, questions such as: " Should all students be required to say the pledge of allegiance?" cannot be submitted to empirical investigation and thus cannot be examined scientifically. Answers to these questions lie in realms other than science.

SCIENTIFIC PRINCIPLE 2
Link Research to Relevant Theory

Scientific theories are, in essence, conceptual models that explain some phenomenon. They are "nets cast to catch what we call 'the world'…we endeavor to make the mesh ever finer and finer" (Popper, 1959, p. 59). Indeed, much of science is fundamentally concerned with developing and testing theories, hypotheses, models, conjectures, or conceptual frameworks that can explain aspects of the physical and social world. Examples of well-known scientific theories include evolution, quantum theory, and the theory of relativity.

In the social sciences and in education, such "grand" theories are rare. To be sure, generalized theoretical understanding is still a goal. However, some research in the social sciences seeks to achieve deep understanding of particular events or circumstances rather than theoretical understanding that will generalize across situations or events. Between these extremes lies the bulk of social science theory or models, what Merton (1973) called

---

[3]Philosophers of science have long debated the meaning of the term empirical. As we state here, in one sense the empirical nature of science means that assertions about the world must be warranted by, or at least constrained by, explicit observation of it. However, we recognize that in addition to direct observation, strategies like logical reasoning and mathematical analysis can also provide empirical support for scientific assertions.

How Can the Cyclic Nature of Ice Ages Be Explained?

During the past 1 billion years, the earth's climate has fluctuated between cold periods, when glaciers scoured the continents, and ice-free warm periods. Serbian mathematician Milutin Milankovitch in the 1930s posited the textbook explanation for these cycles, which was accepted as canon until recently (Milankovitch, 1941/1969; Berger, Imbrie, Hays, Kukla, and Saltzman, 1984). He based his theory on painstaking measurements of the eccentricity—or out-of-roundness—of the Earth's orbit, which changed from almost perfectly circular to slightly oval and back every 100,000 years, matching the interval between glaciation periods. Subsequently, however, analysis of light energy absorbed by Earth, measured from the content of organic material in geological sediment cores, raised doubts about this correlation as a causal mechanism (e.g., MacDonald and Sertorio, 1990). The modest change in eccentricity did not make nearly enough difference in incident sunlight to produce the required change in thermal absorption. Another problem with Milankovitch's explanation was that the geologic record showed some glaciation periods beginning before the orbital changes that supposedly caused them (Broecker, 1992; Winograd, Coplen, and Landwehr, 1992).

Astrophysicist Richard Muller then suggested an alternative mechanism, based on a different aspect of the Earth's orbit (Muller, 1994; Karner and Muller, 2000; also see Grossman, 2001). Muller hypothesized that it is the Earth's orbit in and out of the ecliptic that has been responsible for Earth's cycli-

mid-range theories that attempt to account for some aspect of the social world. Examples of such mid-range theories or explanatory models can be found in the physical and the social sciences.

These theories are representations or abstractions of some aspect of reality that one can only approximate by such models. Molecules, fields, or black holes are classic explanatory models in physics; the genetic code and the contractile filament model of muscle are two in biology. Similarly, cal glaciation periods. He based the hypothesis on astronomical observations showing that the regions above and below the ecliptic are laden with cosmic dust, which would cool the planet. Muller's "inclination theory" received major support when Kenneth Farley (1995) published a paper on cosmic dust in sea sediments.

Farley had begun his research project in an effort to refute the Muller inclination model, but discovered—to his surprise—that cosmic dust levels did indeed wax and wane in sync with the ice ages. As an immediate cause of the temperature change, Muller proposed that dust from space would influence the cloud cover on Earth and the amount of greenhouse gases—mainly carbon dioxide—in the atmosphere. Indeed, measurements of oxygen isotopes in trapped air bubbles and other properties from a 400,000-year-long Antarctic ice core by paleoceanographer Nicholas Shackleton (2001) provided more confirming evidence.

To gain greater understanding of these processes, geochronologists are seeking new "clocks" to determine more accurately the timing of events in the Earth's history (e.g., Feng and Vasconcelos, 2001), while geochemists look for new ways of inferring temperature from composition of gasses trapped deep in ice or rock (see Pope and Giles, 2001). Still, no one knows how orbital variations would send the carbon dioxide into and out of the atmosphere. And there are likely to be other significant geologic factors besides carbon dioxide that control climate. There is much work still to be done to sort out the complex variables that are probably responsible for the ice ages.

culture, socioeconomic status, and poverty are classical models in anthropology, sociology, and political science. In program evaluation, program developers have ideas about the mechanism by which program inputs affect targeted outcomes; evaluations translate and test these ideas through a "program theory" that guides the work (Weiss, 1998a).

Theory enters the research process in two important ways. First, scientific research may be guided by a conceptual framework, model, or theory that suggests possible questions to ask or answers to the question posed.[4] The process of posing significant questions typically occurs before a study is conducted. Researchers seek to test whether a theory holds up under certain circumstances. Here the link between question and theory is straightforward. For example, Putnam based his work on a theoretical conception of institutional performance that related civic engagement and modernization.

A research question can also devolve from a practical problem (Stokes, 1997; see discussion above). In this case, addressing a complex problem like the relationship between class size and student achievement may require several theories. Different theories may give conflicting predictions about the problem's solution, or various theories might have to be reconciled to address the problem. Indeed, the findings from the Tennessee class size reduction study (see Box 3-3) have led to several efforts to devise theoretical understandings of how class size reduction may lead to better student achievement. Scientists are developing models to understand differences in classroom behavior between large and small classes that may ultimately explain and predict changes in achievement (Grissmer and Flannagan, 2000).

A second more subtle way that theoretical understanding factors into the research process derives from the fact that all scientific observations are "theory laden" (Kuhn, 1962). That is, the choice of what to observe and how to observe it is driven by an organizing conception—explicit or tacit—of the problem or topic. Thus, theory drives the research question, the use of methods, and the interpretation of results.

SCIENTIFIC PRINCIPLE 3
Use Methods That Permit Direct Investigation of the Question

Research methods—the design for collecting data and the measurement and analysis of variables in the design—should be selected in light of a research question, and should address it directly. Methods linked directly to problems permit the development of a logical chain of reasoning based

---

[4]The process of posing significant questions or hypotheses may occur, as well, at the end of a study (e.g., Agar, 1996), or over the course of an investigation as understanding of the facets of the problem evolves (e.g., Brown, 1992).

on the interplay among investigative techniques, data, and hypotheses to reach justifiable conclusions. For clarity of discussion, we separate out the link between question and method (see Principle 3) and the rigorous reasoning from evidence to theory (see Principle 4). In the actual practice of research, such a separation cannot be achieved.

Debates about method—in many disciplines and fields—have raged for centuries as researchers have battled over the relative merit of the various techniques of their trade. The simple truth is that the method used to conduct scientific research must fit the question posed, and the investigator must competently implement the method. Particular methods are better suited to address some questions rather than others. The rare choice in the mid 1980s in Tennessee to conduct a randomized field trial, for example, enabled stronger inferences about the effects of class size reduction on student achievement (see Box 3-3) than would have been possible with other methods.

This link between question and method must be clearly explicated and justified; a researcher should indicate how a particular method will enable competent investigation of the question of interest. Moreover, a detailed description of method—measurements, data collection procedures, and data analyses—must be available to permit others to critique or replicate the study (see Principle 5). Finally, investigators should identify potential methodological limitations (such as insensitivity to potentially important variables, missing data, and potential researcher bias).

The choice of method is not always straightforward because, across all disciplines and fields, a wide range of legitimate methods—both quantitative and qualitative—are available to the researcher. For example when considering questions about the natural universe—from atoms to cells to black holes—profoundly different methods and approaches characterize each sub-field. While investigations in the natural sciences are often dependent on the use of highly sophisticated instrumentation (e.g., particle accelerators, gene sequencers, scanning tunneling microscopes), more rudimentary methods often enable significant scientific breakthroughs. For example, in 1995 two Danish zoologists identified an entirely new phylum of animals from a species of tiny rotifer-like creatures found living on the mouthparts of lobsters, using only a hand lens and light microscope (Wilson, 1998, p. 63).

Does Reducing Class Size Improve Students' Achievement?

Although research on the effects of class size reduction on students' achievement dates back 100 years, Glass and Smith (1978) reported the first comprehensive statistical synthesis (meta-analysis) of the literature and concluded that, indeed, there were small improvements in achievement when class size was reduced (see also Glass, Cahen, Smith, and Filby, 1982; Bohrnstedt and Stecher, 1999). However, the Glass and Smith study was criticized (e.g., Robinson and Wittebols, 1986; Slavin, 1989) on a number of grounds, including the selection of some of the studies for the meta-analysis (e.g., tutoring, college classes, atypically small classes). Some subsequent reviews reached conclusions similar to Glass and Smith (e.g., Bohrnstedt and Stetcher, 1999; Hedges, Laine, and Greenwald, 1994; Robinson and Wittebols, 1986) while others did not find consistent evidence of a positive effect (e.g., Hanushek, 1986, 1999a; Odden, 1990; Slavin, 1989).

Does reducing class size improve students' achievement? In the midst of controversy, the Tennessee state legislature asked just this question and funded a randomized experiment to find out, an experiment that Harvard statistician Frederick Mosteller (1995, p. 113) called ". . . one of the most important educational investigations ever carried out." A total of 11,600 elementary school students and their teachers in 79 schools across the state were randomly assigned to one of three class-size conditions: small class (13-17 students), regular class

If a research conjecture or hypothesis can withstand scrutiny by multiple methods its credibility is enhanced greatly. As Webb, Campbell, Schwartz, and Sechrest (1966, pp. 173-174) phrased it: "When a hypothesis can survive the confrontation of a series of complementary methods of testing, it contains a degree of validity unattainable by one tested within the more constricted framework of a single method." Putnam's study (see Box 3-1) provides an example in which both quantitative and qualitative methods were applied in a longitudinal design (e.g., interview, survey, statistical estimate of institutional performance, analysis of legislative docu-

(22-26 students), or regular class (22-26 students) with a full-time teacher's aide (for descriptions of the experiment, see Achilles, 1999; Finn and Achilles, 1990; Folger and Breda, 1989; Krueger, 1999; Word et al., 1990). The experiment began with a cohort of students who entered kindergarten in 1985, and lasted 4 years. After third grade, all students returned to regular size classes. Although students were supposed to stay in their original treatment conditions for four years, not all did. Some were randomly reassigned between regular and regular/aide conditions in the first grade while about 10 percent switched between conditions for other reasons (Krueger and Whitmore, 2000).

Three findings from this experiment stand out. First, students in small classes outperformed students in regular size classes (with or without aides). Second, the benefits of class-size reduction were much greater for minorities (primarily African American) and inner-city children than others (see, e.g., Finn and Achilles, 1990, 1999; but see also Hanushek, 1999b). And third, even though students returned to regular classes in fourth grade, the reduced class-size effect persisted in affecting whether they took college entrance examinations and on their examination performance (Krueger and Whitmore, 2001).*

---

*Interestingly, in balancing the size of the effects of class size reduction with the costs, the Tennessee legislature decided *not* to reduce class size in the state (Ritter and Boruch, 1999).

ments) to generate converging evidence about the effects of modernization on civic community. New theories about the periodicity of the ice ages, similarly, were informed by multiple methods (e.g., astronomical observations of cosmic dust, measurements of oxygen isotopes). The integration and interaction of multiple disciplinary perspectives—with their varying methods—often accounts for scientific progress (Wilson, 1998); this is evident, for example, in the advances in understanding early reading skills described in Chapter 2. This line of work features methods that range from neuroimaging to qualitative classroom observation.

We close our discussion of this principle by noting that in many sciences, measurement is a key aspect of research method. This is true for many research endeavors in the social sciences and education research, although not for all of them. If the concepts or variables are poorly specified or inadequately measured, even the best methods will not be able to support strong scientific inferences. The history of the natural sciences is one of remarkable development of concepts and variables, as well as the tools (instrumentation) to measure them. Measurement reliability and validity is particularly challenging in the social sciences and education (Messick, 1989). Sometimes theory is not strong enough to permit clear specification and justification of the concept or variable. Sometimes the tool (e.g., multiple-choice test) used to take the measurement seriously under-represents the construct (e.g., science achievement) to be measured. Sometimes the use of the measurement has an unintended social consequence (e.g., the effect of teaching to the test on the scope of the curriculum in schools).

And sometimes error is an inevitable part of the measurement process. In the physical sciences, many phenomena can be directly observed or have highly predictable properties; measurement error is often minimal. (However, see National Research Council [1991] for a discussion of when and how measurement in the physical sciences can be imprecise.) In sciences that involve the study of humans, it is essential to identify those aspects of measurement error that attenuate the estimation of the relationships of interest (e.g., Shavelson, Baxter, and Gao, 1993). By investigating those aspects of a social measurement that give rise to measurement error, the measurement process itself will often be improved. Regardless of field of study, scientific measurements should be accompanied by estimates of uncertainty whenever possible (see Principle 4 below).

SCIENTIFIC PRINCIPLE 4
Provide Coherent, Explicit Chain of Reasoning

The extent to which the inferences that are made in the course of scientific work are warranted depends on rigorous reasoning that systematically and logically links empirical observations with the underlying theory and the degree to which both the theory and the observations are linked to the question or problem that lies at the root of the investigation. There is no recipe for determining how these ingredients should be combined; instead, what is required is the development of a logical "chain of reasoning" (Lesh, Lovitts, and Kelly, 2000) that moves from evidence to theory and back again. This chain of reasoning must be coherent, explicit (one that another researcher could replicate), and persuasive to a skeptical reader (so that, for example, counterhypotheses are addressed).

All rigorous research—quantitative and qualitative—embodies the same underlying logic of inference (King, Keohane, and Verba, 1994). This inferential reasoning is supported by clear statements about how the research conclusions were reached: What assumptions were made? How was evidence judged to be relevant? How were alternative explanations considered or discarded? How were the links between data and the conceptual or theoretical framework made?

The nature of this chain of reasoning will vary depending on the design of the study, which in turn will vary depending on the question that is being investigated. Will the research develop, extend, modify, or test a hypothesis? Does it aim to determine: *What* works? *How* does it work? *Under what circumstances* does it work? If the goal of the research is to test a hypothesis, stated in the form of an "if-then" rule, successful inference may depend on measuring the extent to which the rule predicts results under a variety of conditions. If the goal is to produce a description of a complex system, such as a subcellular organelle or a hierarchical social organization, successful inference may rather depend on issues of fidelity and internal consistency of the observational techniques applied to diverse components and the credibility of the evidence gathered. The research design and the inferential reasoning it enables must demonstrate a thorough understanding of the subtleties of the questions to be asked and the procedures used to answer them.

Muller (1994), for example, collected data on the inclination of the Earth's orbit over a 100,000 year cycle, correlated it with the occurrence of ice ages, ruled out the plausibility of orbital eccentricity as a cause for the occurrence of ice ages, and inferred that the bounce in the Earth's orbit likely caused the ice ages (see Box 3-2). Putnam used multiple methods to subject to rigorous testing his hypotheses about what affects the success or failure of democratic institutions as they develop in diverse social environments to rigorous testing, and found the weight of the evidence favored the assertion that civic tradition matters more than economic affluence (see Box 3-1). And Baumeister, Bratslavsky, Muraven, and Tice (1998) compared three competing theories and used randomized experiments to conclude that a "psychic energy" hypothesis best explained the important psychological characteristic of "will power" (see "Application of the Principles").

This principle has several features worthy of elaboration. Assumptions underlying the inferences made should be clearly stated and justified. Moreover, choice of design should both acknowledge potential biases and plan for implementation challenges.

Estimates of error must also be made. Claims to knowledge vary substantially according to the strength of the research design, theory, and control of extraneous variables and by systematically ruling out possible alternative explanations. Although scientists always reason in the presence of uncertainty, it is critical to gauge the magnitude of this uncertainty. In the physical and life sciences, quantitative estimates of the error associated with conclusions are often computed and reported. In the social sciences and education, such quantitative measures are sometimes difficult to generate; in any case, a statement about the nature and estimated magnitude of error must be made in order to signal the level of certainty with which conclusions have been drawn.

Perhaps most importantly, the reasoning about evidence should identify, consider, and incorporate, when appropriate, the alternative, competing explanations or rival "answers" to the research question. To make valid inferences, plausible counterexplanations must be dealt with in a rational, systematic, and compelling way.[5] The validity—or credibility—of a hypothesis is substantially strengthened if alternative counterhypotheses can be ruled out and the favored one thereby supported. Well-known research designs (e.g., Campbell and Stanley [1963] in educational psychology; Heckman [1979, 1980a, 1980b, 2001] and Goldberger [1972, 1983] in

---

[5]In reporting, too, it is important to clarify that rival hypotheses are possible and that conclusions are not presented as if they were gospel. Murphy and colleagues call this "'fair-dealing'—wariness of presenting the perspective of one group as if it defined a single truth about the phenomenon, while paying scant attention to other perspectives" (Murphy, Dingwall, Greatbatch, Parker, and Watson, 1998, p. 192).

economics; and Rosenbaum and Rubin [1983, 1984] in statistics) have been crafted to guard researchers against specific counterhypotheses (or "threats to validity"). One example, often called "selectivity bias," is the counterhypothesis that differential selection (not the treatment) caused the outcome—that participants in the experimental treatment systematically differed from participants in the traditional (control) condition in ways that mattered importantly to the outcome. A cell biologist, for example, might unintentionally place (select) heart cells with a slight glimmer into an experimental group and others into a control group, thus potentially biasing the comparison between the groups of cells. The potential for a biased—or unfair—comparison arises because the shiny cells could differ systematically from the others in ways that affect what is being studied.

Selection bias is a pervasive problem in the social sciences and education research. To illustrate, in studying the effects of class-size reduction, credentialed teachers are more likely to be found in wealthy school districts that have the resources to reduce class size than in poor districts. This fact raises the possibility that higher achievement will be observed in the smaller classes due to factors other than class size (e.g.. teacher effects). Random assignment to "treatment" is the strongest known antidote to the problem of selection bias (see Chapter 5).

A second counterhypothesis contends that something in the research participants' history that co-occurred with the treatment caused the outcome, not the treatment itself. For example, U.S. fourth-grade students outperformed students in others countries on the ecology subtest of the Third International Mathematics and Science Study. One (popular) explanation of this finding was that the effect was due to their schooling and the emphasis on ecology in U.S. elementary science curricula. A counterhypothesis, one of history, posits that their high achievement was due to the prevalence of ecology in children's television programming. A control group that has the same experiences as the experimental group except for the "treatment" under study is the best antidote for this problem.

A third prevalent class of alternative interpretations contends that an outcome was biased by the measurement used. For example, education effects are often judged by narrowly defined achievement tests that focus on factual knowledge and therefore favor direct-instruction teaching techniques. Multiple achievement measures with high reliability (consistency) and validity (accuracy) help to counter potential measurement bias.

The Tennessee class-size study was designed primarily to eliminate all possible known explanations, except for reduced class size, in comparing the achievement of children in regular classrooms against achievement in reduced size classrooms. It did this. Complications remained, however. About ten percent of students moved out of their originally assigned condition (class size), weakening the design because the comparative groups did not remain intact to enable strict comparisons. However, most scholars who subsequently analyzed the data (e.g., Krueger and Whitmore, 2001), while limited by the original study design, suggested that these infidelities did not affect the main conclusions of the study that smaller class size caused slight improvements in achievement. Students in classes of 13-17 students outperformed their peers in larger classes, on average, by a small margin.

SCIENTIFIC PRINCIPLE 5
Replicate and Generalize Across Studies

Replication and generalization strengthen and clarify the limits of scientific conjectures and theories. By replication we mean, at an elementary level, that if one investigator makes a set of observations, another investigator can make a similar set of observations under the same conditions. Replication in this sense comes close to what psychometricians call reliability—consistency of measurements from one observer to another, from one task to another parallel task, from one occasion to another occasion. Estimates of these different types of reliability can vary when measuring a given construct: for example, in measuring performance of military personnel (National Research Council, 1991), multiple observers largely agreed on what they observed within tasks; however, enlistees' performance across parallel tasks was quite inconsistent.

At a somewhat more complex level, replication means the ability to repeat an investigation in more than one setting (from one laboratory to another or from one field site to a similar field site) and reach similar conclusions. To be sure, replication in the physical sciences, especially with inanimate objects, is more easily achieved than in social science or education; put another way, the margin of error in social science replication is usually much greater than in physical science replication. The role of contextual factors and the lack of control that characterizes work in the social realm require a more nuanced notion of replication. Nevertheless, the typically large margins of error in social science replications do not preclude their identification.

Having evidence of replication, an important goal of science is to understand the extent to which findings generalize from one object or person to another, from one setting to another, and so on. To this end, a substantial amount of statistical machinery has been built both to help ensure that what is observed in a particular study is representative of what is of larger interest (i.e., will generalize) and to provide a quantitative measure of the possible error in generalizing. Nonstatistical means of generalization (e.g., triangulation, analytic induction, comparative analysis) have also been developed and applied in genres of research, such as ethnography, to understand the extent to which findings generalize across time, space, and populations. Subsequent applications, implementations, or trials are often necessary to assure generalizability or to clarify its limits. For example, since the Tennessee experiment, additional studies of the effects of class size reduction on student learning have been launched in settings other than Tennessee to assess the extent to which the findings generalize (e.g., Hruz, 2000).

In the social sciences and education, many generalizations are limited to particular times and particular places (Cronbach, 1975). This is because the social world undergoes rapid and often significant change; social generalizations, as Cronbach put it, have a shorter "half-life" than those in the physical world. Campbell and Stanley (1963) dubbed the extent to which the treatment conditions and participant population of a study mirror the world to which generalization is desired the "external validity" of the study. Consider, again, the Tennessee class-size research; it was undertaken in a set of schools that had the desire to participate, the physical facilities to accommodate an increased number of classrooms, and adequate teaching staff. Governor Wilson of California "overgeneralized" the Tennessee study, ignoring the specific experimental conditions of will and capacity and implemented class-size reduction in more than 95 percent of grades K-3 in the state. Not surprisingly, most researchers studying California have concluded that the Tennessee findings did not entirely generalize to a different time, place, and context (see, e.g., Stecher and Bohrnstedt, 2000).[6]

SCIENTIFIC PRINCIPLE 6
Disclose Research to Encourage Professional Scrutiny and Critique

We argue in Chapter 2 that a characteristic of scientific knowledge accumulation is its contested nature. Here we suggest that science is not only characterized by professional scrutiny and criticism, but also that such criticism is *essential* to scientific progress. Scientific studies usually are elements of a larger corpus of work; furthermore, the scientists carrying out a particular study always are part of a larger community of scholars. Reporting and reviewing research results are essential to enable wide and meaningful peer review. Results are traditionally published in a specialty journal, in books published by academic presses, or in other peer-reviewed publications. In recent years, an electronic version may accompany or even substitute for a print publication.[7] Results may be debated at professional conferences. Regardless of the medium, the goals of research reporting are to communicate the findings from the investigation; to open the study to examination, criticism, review, and replication (see Principle 5) by peer investigators; and ultimately to incorporate the new knowledge into the prevailing canon of the field.[8]

---

[6]A question arises as to whether this is a failure to generalize or a problem of poor implementation. The conditions under which Tennessee implemented the experiment were not reproduced in California with the now known consequence of failure to replicate and generalize.

[7]The committee is concerned that the quality of peer review in electronic modes of dissemination varies greatly and sometimes cannot be easily assessed from its source. While the Internet is providing new and exciting ways to connect scientists and promote scientific debate, the extent to which the principles of science are met in some electronically posted work is often unclear.

[8]Social scientists and education researchers also commonly publish information about new knowledge for practitioners and the public. In those cases, the research must be reported in accessible ways so that readers can understand the researcher's procedures and evaluate the evidence, interpretations, and arguments.

The goal of communicating new knowledge is self-evident: research results must be brought into the professional and public domain if they are to be understood, debated, and eventually become known to those who could fruitfully use them. The extent to which new work can be reviewed and challenged by professional peers depends critically on accurate, comprehensive, and accessible records of data, method, and inferential reasoning. This careful accounting not only makes transparent the reasoning that led to conclusions—promoting its credibility—but it also allows the community of scientists and analysts to comprehend, to replicate, and otherwise to inform theory, research, and practice in that area.

Many nonscientists who seek guidance from the research community bemoan what can easily be perceived as bickering or as an indication of "bad" science. Quite the contrary: intellectual debate at professional meetings, through research collaborations, and in other settings provide the means by which scientific knowledge is refined and accepted; scientists strive for an "open society" where criticism and unfettered debate point the way to advancement. Through scholarly critique (see, e.g., Skocpol, 1996) and debate, for example, Putnam's work has stimulated a series of articles, commentary, and controversy in research and policy circles about the role of "social capital" in political and other social phenomena (Winter, 2000). And the Tennessee class size study has been the subject of much scholarly debate, leading to a number of follow-on analyses and launching new work that attempts to understand the process by which classroom behavior may shift in small classes to facilitate learning. However, as Lagemann (2000) has observed, for many reasons the education research community has not been nearly as critical of itself as is the case in other fields of scientific study.

APPLICATION OF THE PRINCIPLES

The committee considered a wide range of literature and scholarship to test its ideas about the guiding principles. We realized, for example, that empiricism, while a hallmark of science, does not uniquely define it. A poet can write from first-hand experience of the world, and in this sense is an empiricist. And making observations of the world, and reasoning about their experience, helps both literary critics and historians create the interpretive frameworks that they bring to bear in their scholarship. But empirical method in scientific inquiry has different features, like codified procedures for making observations and recognizing sources of bias associated with particular methods,[9] and the data derived from these observations are used specifically as tools to support or refute knowledge claims. Finally, empiricism in science involves collective judgments based on logic, experience, and consensus.

Another hallmark of science is replication and generalization. Humanists do not seek replication, although they often attempt to create work that generalizes (say) to the "human condition." However, they have no formal logic of generalization, unlike scientists working in some domains (e.g., statistical sampling theory). In sum, it is clear that there is no bright line that distinguishes science from nonscience or high-quality science from low-quality science. Rather, our principles can be used as general guidelines for understanding what can be considered scientific and what can be considered high-quality science (see, however, Chapters 4 and 5 for an elaboration).

To show how our principles help differentiate science from other forms of scholarship, we briefly consider two genres of education inquiry published in refereed journals and books. We do *not* make a judgment about the worth of either form of inquiry; although we believe strongly in the merits of scientific inquiry in education research and more generally, that "science" does not mean "good." Rather, we use them as examples to illustrate the distinguishing character of our principles of science. The first—*connoisseurship*—grew out of the arts and humanities (e.g., Eisner, 1991) and does not claim to be scientific. The second—*portraiture*—claims to straddle the fence between humanistic and scientific inquiry (e.g., Lawrence-Lightfoot and Davis, 1997).

Eisner (1991, p. 7) built a method for education inquiry firmly rooted in the arts and humanities, arguing that "there are multiple ways in which the world can be known: Artists, writers, and dancers, as well as scientists, have important things to tell about the world." His method of inquiry combines connoisseurship (the art of appreciation), which "aims to

---

[9]We do not claim that any one investigator or observational method is "objective." Rather, the guiding principles are established to guard against bias through rigorous methods and a critical community.

appreciate the qualities . . . that constitute an act, work, or object and, typically . . . to relate these to the contextual and antecedent conditions" (p. 85) with educational criticism (the art of disclosure), which provides "connoisseurship with a public face" (p. 85). The goal of this genre of research is to enable readers to enter an event and to participate in it. To this end, the educational critic—through educational connoisseurship— must capture the key qualities of the material, situation, and experience and express them in text ("criticism") to make what the critic sees clear to others. "To know what schools are like, their strengths and their weaknesses, we need to be able to *see* what occurs in them, and we need to be able to tell others what we have seen in ways that are vivid and insightful" (Eisner, 1991, p. 23, italics in original).

The grounds for his knowledge claims are not those in our guiding principles. Rather, credibility is established by: (1) structural corroboration—"multiple types of data are related to each other" (p. 110) and "*disconfirming evidence and contradictory interpretations*" (p. 111; italics in original) are considered; (2) consensual validation—"agreement among competent others that the description, interpretation, evaluation, and thematics of an educational situation are right" (p. 112); and (3) referential adequacy—"the extent to which a reader is able to locate in its subject matter the qualities the critic addresses and the meanings he or she ascribes to these" (p. 114). While sharing some features of our guiding principles (e.g., ruling out counterinterpretations to the favored interpretation), this humanistic approach to knowledge claims builds on a very different epistemology; the key scientific concepts of reliability, replication, and generalization, for example, are quite different. We agree with Eisner that such approaches fall outside the purview of science and conclude that our guiding principles readily distinguish them.

Portraiture (Lawrence-Lightfoot, 1994; Lawrence-Lightfoot and Davis, 1997) is a qualitative research method that aims to "record and interpret the perspectives and experience of the people they [the researchers] are studying, documenting their [the research participants'] voices and their visions—their authority, knowledge, and wisdom" (Lawrence-Lightfoot and Davis, 1997, p. xv). In contrast to connoisseurship's humanist orientation, portraiture "seeks to join science and art" (Lawrence-Lightfoot and Davis, 1997, p. xv) by "embracing the intersection of aesthetics and empiricism" (p. 6). The standard for judging the quality of portraiture is authenticity,

". . . capturing the essence and resonance of the actors' experience and perspective through the details of action and thought revealed in context" (p. 12). When empirical and literary themes come together (called "resonance") for the researcher, the actors, and the audience, "we speak of the portrait as achieving authenticity" (p. 260).

In *I've Known Rivers*, Lawrence-Lightfoot (1994) explored the life stories of six men and women:

> . . . using the intensive, probing method of 'human archeology'—a name I [Lawrence-Lightfoot] coined for this genre of portraiture as a way of trying to convey the depth and penetration of the inquiry, the richness of the layers of human experience, the search for ancestral and generational artifacts, and the painstaking, careful labor that the metaphorical dig requires. As I listen to the life stories of these individuals and participate in the 'co-construction' of narrative, I employ the themes, goals, and techniques of portraiture. It is an eclectic, interdisciplinary approach, shaped by the lenses of history, anthropology, psychology and sociology. I blend the curiosity and detective work of a biographer, the literary aesthetic of a novelist, and the systematic scrutiny of a researcher (p. 15).

Some scholars, then, deem portraiture as "scientific" because it relies on the use of social science theory and a form of empiricism (e.g., interview). While both empiricism and theory are important elements of our guiding principles, as we discuss above, they are not, in themselves, defining. The devil is in the details. For example, independent replication is an important principle in our framework but is absent in portraiture in which researcher and subject jointly construct a narrative. Moreover, even when our principles are manifest, the specific form and mode of application can make a big difference. For example, generalization in our principles is different from generalization in portraiture. As Lawrence-Lightfoot and Davis (1997) point out, generalization as used in the social sciences does not fit portraiture. Generalization in portraiture ". . . is not the classical conception . . . where the investigator uses codified methods for generalizing from specific findings to a universe, and where there is little interest in findings that reflect only the characteristics of the sample. . . ." By contrast, the portraitist seeks to "document and illuminate the complexity and detail of a unique experience or place, hoping the audience will see itself reflected in it, trusting that the readers will feel identified. The portraitist is very interested in the single case because she believes that embedded in it the reader will discover resonant universal themes" (p. 15). We conclude that our guiding principles would distinguish portraiture from what we mean by scientific inquiry, although it, like connoisseurship, has some traits in common.

To this point, we have shown how our principles help to distinguish science and nonscience. A large amount of education research attempts to base knowledge claims on science; clearly, however, there is great variation with respect to scientific rigor and competence. Here we use two studies to illustrate how our principles demonstrate this gradation in scientific quality.

The first study (Carr, Levin, McConnachie, Carlson, Kemp, Smith, and McLaughlin, 1999) reported on an educational intervention carried out on three nonrandomly selected individuals who were suffering severe behavioral disorders and who were either residing in group-home settings or with their parents. Since earlier work had established remedial procedures involving "simulations and analogs of the natural environment" (p. 6), the focus of the study was on the generalizability (or external validity) to the "real world" of the intervention (places, caregivers).

Using a multiple baseline design, baseline frequencies of their problem behaviors were established, and these behaviors were remeasured while an intervention lasting for some years was carried out. The researchers also took several measurements during the maintenance phase of the study. While care was taken in describing behavioral observations, variable construction and reliability, the paper reporting on the study did not provide clear, detailed depictions of the interventions or who carried them out (research staff, staff of the group homes, or family members). Furthermore, no details were given of the changes in staffing or in the regimens of the residential settings—changes that were inevitable over a period of many years (the timeline itself was not clearly described). Finally, in the course of daily life over a number of years, many things would have happened to each of the subjects, some of which might be expected to be of significance to the study, but none of them were documented. Over the years, too, one might expect some developmental changes to occur in the aggressive behavior displayed by the research subjects, especially in the two teenagers. In short, the study focused on generalizability at too great an expense relative to internal validity. In the end, there were many threats to internal validity in this study, and so it is impossible to conclude (as the authors did) from the published report that the "treatment" had actually caused the improvement in behavior that was noted.

Turning to a line of work that we regard as scientifically more successful, in a series of four randomized experiments, Baumeister, Bratslavsky, Muraven, and Tice (1998) tested three competing theories of "will power" (or, more technically, "self-regulation")—the psychological characteristic that is posited to be related to persistence with difficult tasks such as studying or working on homework assignments. One hypothesis was that will power is a developed skill that would remain roughly constant across repeated trials. The second theory posited a self-control schema "that makes use of information about how to alter one's own response" (p. 1254) so that once activated on one trial, it would be expected to increase will power on a second trial. The third theory, anticipated by Freud's notion of the ego exerting energy to control the id and superego, posits that will power is a depletable resource—it requires the use of "psychic energy" so that performance from trial 1 to trial 2 would decrease if a great deal of will power was called for on trial 1. In one experiment, 67 introductory psychology students were randomly assigned to a condition in which either no food was present or both radishes and freshly baked chocolate chip cookies were present, and the participants were instructed either to eat two or three radishes (resisting the cookies) or two or three cookies (resisting the radishes). Immediately following this situation, all participants were asked to work on two puzzles that unbeknownst to them, were unsolvable, and their persistence (time) in working on the puzzles was measured. The experimental manipulation was checked for every individual participating by researchers observing their behavior through a one-way window. The researchers found that puzzle persistence was the same in the control and cookie conditions and about 2.5 times as long, on average, as in the radish condition, lending support to the psychic energy theory—arguably, resisting the temptation to eat the cookies evidently had depleted the reserve of self-control, leading to poor performance on the second task. Later experiments extended the findings supporting the energy theory to situations involving choice, maladaptive performance, and decision making.

However, as we have said, no single study or series of studies satisfy all of our guiding principles, and these will power experiments are no exception. They all employed small samples of participants, all drawn from a college population. The experiments were contrived—the conditions of the study would be unlikely outside a psychology laboratory. And the question of whether these findings would generalize to more realistic (e.g., school) settings was not addressed.

Nevertheless, the contrast in quality between the two studies, when observed through the lens of our guiding principles, is stark. Unlike the first study, the second study was grounded in theory and identified three competing answers to the question of self-regulation, each leading to a different empirically refutable claim. In doing so, the chain of reasoning was made transparent. The second study, unlike the first, used randomized experiments to address counterclaims to the inference of psychic energy, such as selectivity bias or different history during experimental sessions. Finally, in the second study, the series of experiments replicated and extended the effects hypothesized by the energy theory.

CONCLUDING COMMENT

Nearly a century ago, John Dewey (1916) captured the essence of the account of science we have developed in this chapter and expressed a hopefulness for the promise of science we similarly embrace:

> Our predilection for premature acceptance and assertion, our aversion to suspended judgment, are signs that we tend naturally to cut short the process of testing. We are satisfied with superficial and immediate short-visioned applications. If these work out with moderate satisfactoriness, we are content to suppose that our assumptions have been confirmed. Even in the case of failure, we are inclined to put the blame not on the inadequacy and incorrectness of our data and thoughts, but upon our hard luck and the hostility of circumstances. . . . Science represents the safeguard of the [human] race against these natural propensities and the evils which flow from them. It consists of the special appliances and methods... slowly worked out in order to conduct reflection under conditions whereby its procedures and results are tested.

4

Features of Education and Education Research

In Chapter 3 the committee argues that the guiding principles for scientific research in education are the same as those in the social, physical, and life sciences. Yet the ways that those principles are instantiated—in astrophysics, biochemistry, labor economics, cultural anthropology, or mathematics teaching—depend on the specific features of what is being studied. That is, each field has features that influence what questions are asked, how research is designed, how it is carried out, and how it is interpreted and generalized. Scholars working in a particular area establish the traditions and standards for how to most appropriately apply the guiding principles to their area of study (Diamond, 1999).

In this chapter, we describe how our principles of science translate in the study of education—a rich tapestry of teaching, learning, and schooling. In particular, we briefly discuss five features of *education* that shape scientific inquiry, and describe how these features affect research. We argue that a key implication of these features of education is the need to account for influential contextual factors within the process of inquiry and in understanding the extent to which findings can be generalized. These features sharpen the conception of scientific research quality we develop in Chapter 3. We also discuss three features of *education research* that are essential to understanding the nature and conduct of the professional work.

To set the stage for our discussion of the particulars of scientific education research, we reiterate our position that there are substantial similarities between inquiry in the physical and social worlds. We have argued in previous chapters that our principles of science are common across disciplines and fields and that the accumulation of knowledge progresses in roughly the same way. Furthermore, profoundly different methods and approaches characterize each discipline and field in the physical sciences, depending on such things as the time frame, the scale of magnitude, and the complexity of the instrumentation required. The same is true in the social sciences and education, where questions ranging from individual learning of varied subject matter to fundamental social patterns to cultural norms determine the length of time, the number of people, and the kind of research instruments that are needed in conducting the studies.

Differences in the phenomena typically under investigation do distinguish the research conducted by physical and social scientists. For example, the social and cultural work of sociologists and cultural anthropologists often do not lend themselves to the controlled conditions, randomized treatments, or repeated measures that typify investigations in physics or chemistry. Phenomena such as language socialization, deviancy, the development of an idea, or the interaction of cultural tradition with educational instruction are notoriously impervious to the controls used in the systematic investigations of atoms or molecules. Unlike atoms or molecules, people grow up and change over time. The social, cultural, and economic conditions they experience evolve with history. The abstract concepts and ideas that are meaningful to them vary across time, space, and cultural tradition. These circumstances have led some social science and education researchers to investigative approaches that look distinctly different from those of physical researchers, while still aligning with the guiding principles outlined in Chapter 3.

Another area that can notably distinguish research between the social and physical sciences concerns researcher objectivity in relation to bias. In some physical and life sciences, investigators are often deliberately kept ignorant of the identity of research participants, and controls are instituted through such devices as double-blind or randomization procedures. This strategy is often used in medical trials to ensure that researchers' perspectives are not influenced by their knowledge of which participants received which treatment, and similarly, that this knowledge does not alter the behavior of the research participants. In many areas of the social sciences, in contrast, the investigator is recognized as an "engaged participant observer," involved with the experience and action of those observed (Blumer, 1966; Denzin, 1978; Kelly and Lesh, 2000). In such "naturalistic research paradigms" (Moschkovich and Brenner, 2000), investigators do not seek to distance themselves from research participants, but rather to immerse themselves in the participants' lives, with conscious attention to how the investigator affects and contributes to the research process. Such strategies were developed to allow the researcher to observe, analyze, and integrate into the research process unexpected, constantly changing, and other potentially influential aspects of what is being studied. These approaches are often particularly important in studying how changes in school subject matter or the development of new technologies can be incorporated into educational practice. In collecting and coding such qualitative data, convergence can be demonstrated with repeated instances, more than one observer, and multiple raters. Also essential to the process is the examination of competing interpretations, contrasting cases, and disconfirming evidence. Regularity in the patterns across groups and across time—rather than replication per se—is a source of generalization. The goal of such scientific methods, of course, remains the same: to identify generalized patterns.

Uses of theory also tend to distinguish work in the social and physical sciences. Theory in the physical sciences leads to predictions about things that will happen in the future. Strong theories include causal mechanisms that predict what will happen and give insights into why. Theory in the social sciences is predictive, but more often it serves to understand things that happened in the past, serving a more diagnostic or explanatory purpose. Understanding the past often enables social science researchers to explain why things happened. Though understanding the past can sometimes predict the future, it does so only in broad outline and with a lesser degree of certainty. For instance, researchers have documented the regularity of certain misconceptions and patterns of error as students learn scientific or mathematical ideas. Although one cannot predict exactly when they will occur, awareness of them permits teachers to interpret student comments more effectively and to create assessment items to test for evidence of them.

A related and final point is that the level of certainty with which research conclusions can be made is typically higher in the physical sciences than in the social sciences. As we discuss in Chapter 3, many scientific claims have some degree of uncertainty associated with them—that is, they are probabilistic rather than deterministic. We include within our principles the idea that careful estimation and reporting of uncertainty is crucial to science. However, because theories that model social phenomena—human behavior, ideas, cultures—are not as well developed as those for some physical phenomena and because they are often out of the direct control of the researcher, results are always probabilistic and tend to be more tentative than in the physical sciences. In technical terms, this means that the "error limits" associated with scientific inferences (not unlike confidence intervals typically cited in public opinion polls) tend to be larger in social and behavioral research, often due to the "noise" caused by difficulties precisely measuring key constructs and major contextual factors. The influential role of context in many social and behavioral research inquiries is a fundamental aspect of studying humans. However, it does make replication—the key to boosting certainty in results and refining theory—more difficult and nuanced. In sum, the degree of precision associated with current social science findings tends to be lower than that in the physical and life sciences.

Although education research has its roots in the social and behavioral sciences, it is also an applied field—akin in important ways to medicine and agriculture. Some scholars have likened education research to the engineering sciences, arguing that it is an enterprise fundamentally aimed at bringing theoretical understanding to practical problem solving. Like other applied fields, education research serves two related purposes: to add to fundamental understanding of education-related phenomena and events, and to inform practical decision making. Both are worthy, both require researchers to have a keen understanding of educational practice and policy, and both can ultimately lead to improvements in practice. Education research with the sole aim of explaining, describing, or predicting closely resembles "traditional" scientific inquiry of the kind we describe in the previous chapter. Research whose direct aim is to aid educational practice, decision making, and policy in the near term also must meet scientific principles for rigor, but it has an action orientation. The dual purposes of education research suggest that there must be a balance of considerations of the factors of the validity of the knowledge claims, the credibility of the research team, and the utility and relevance of the work to situations of educational practice.

Scientific education research, whether it is aimed primarily at uncovering new knowledge or meeting the dual goals of generating knowledge and informing practice, is influenced by the unique configuration of characteristic features of the educational enterprise.

FEATURES OF EDUCATION

Education is a complex human endeavor ultimately aimed at enhancing students' cognitive, civic, and social learning and development. Like medicine, law, or farming, education is a craft—a practical profession requiring specialized skill. Researchers studying teachers have documented that teaching is a complex, interactive exchange as the teachers seek to engage students in learning new matieral; to relate it to their prior knowledge; to respond to the heterogeneous needs of children with varied backgrounds, interests, and ideas; and to assess the depth and endurance of student learning. Education can occur in school classrooms, private homes, museums, community centers and through information accessible on the Web. Even formal schooling varies in profound ways from community to community, and from preschoolers to adults. Its institutions are many and multilayered—elementary schools, middle schools, high schools, 2-year and vocational colleges, 4-year colleges and universities, and adult learning centers. As an institution, its clientele frequently move, for example, from one school or college to another. The variability and complexity of education is mirrored by the practice of education. In the exercise of their craft, educators draw on, and are influenced by, practical wisdom, professional relationships, and values, as well as scientifically grounded theory and fact. Indeed, it is this real world of research in education that led columnist Miller to lament, "If only education reforms came in a pill" (2001, p. A14).

The character of education not only affects the research enterprise, but also necessitates careful consideration of how the understanding or use of results can be impeded or facilitated by conditions at different levels of the system. Organizational, structural, and leadership qualities all influence how the complex education system works in practice. Results may have "shelf lives" that vary with cultural shifts and resource changes (Cronbach, 1975).

In the section that follows we discuss some of the salient features of education and their effects on scientific research: values and politics; human volition; variability in education programs; the organization of schools; and the diversity of the many individuals involved in education.

Values and Politics

Aristotle once opined that it is impossible to talk about education apart from some conception of "the good life" (Cremin, 1990, p. 85). Indeed, education is a field in which values appropriately play a central role, because what people hope to attain in education—especially the education of children—is intimately connected with people's views about individual human potential, their hopes and expectations of what society can become, and their ideas about how social problems can be alleviated. In this way, social ideals inevitably and properly influence the education system and in turn, the research that is carried out. More subtly, but crucially, these values also affect the choice of outcomes to study and measure, as they are proxies for the myriad goals of education: basic knowledge and skills, community service, job training, social development, and problem solving. We comment further on the implications of these disagreements about goals in discussing the role of a federal education research agency in Chapter 6.

A more global implication of the role of values in education research concerns the extent to which research in education is truly akin to an engineering science. The question of why education research has not produced the equivalent of a Salk vaccine is telling. After all, medical research is something of an engineering science in that it brings theoretical understanding in the life sciences to bear on solving the practical problems of prolonging life and reducing disease. Education research is similar, with the key difference that there is less consensus on the goal. Medical research often has clearer goals—for example, finding a cure for cancer. Because values are so deeply embedded in education in so many different ways, education researchers do not have a singular practical goal that drives their inquiry (Bruner, 1996).

Local, state, and federal politicians, teacher unions, special interest groups, higher education faculty, and other interested citizens who have a stake in education are often moving in different directions and driven by different sets of incentives. These stakeholders make decisions that influence education policy and practice, and thus have an impact on the research that attempts to model and understand it. At any given time, schools and school systems may be responding to a configuration of possibly conflicting demands from these stakeholders, while trying to serve their primary clients—children, parents, and community members. This dynamic creates a turbulent environment for research. Furthermore, political motivations can affect the uses of research; some stakeholders may have strong incentives to resist the findings or interpretations of researchers or to over-interpret the results if they indicate even modest degrees of evidentiary support.

Another potential consequence of the role of stakeholders is that education research can be interrupted by a change in policy or political support for a particular type of reform. In California, the mathematics and science standards crafted in the late 1980s—which served as important examples for the current national mathematics and science standards—were abruptly changed because of political shifts. Just as the state was gearing up its curriculum, teaching, and accountability system to implement the new standards in a systematic way, the political environment changed, and so did the standards and accountability system (Kirst and Mazzeo, 1996). Research on the reform, too, ended abruptly. Such changes occur as a result of the democratic system of educational governance in the United States, and can have practical implications for research planning (e.g., limiting opportunities to conduct long-term studies).

Human Volition

Education is centrally concerned with people: learners, teachers, parents, citizens, and policy makers. The volition, or will, of these individuals decreases the level of control that researchers can have over the process. For example, in some cases, people cannot be randomly assigned to treatment groups; they will not agree to let themselves or their children be "controlled" for the purposes of experimental trials. This lack of control can also cause problems of noncompliance with research protocols and instances of missing data because, for example, parents have the interests of their individual child in mind and may have priorities and needs that conflict with those of the research process.

Human movement and change have, for example, affected efforts to study the effects of education vouchers on student achievement. Many voucher studies (Witte, 2000; Peterson, 1998; Rouse, 1997; Peterson, Howell, and Greene, 1999; Myers, Peterson, Mayer, Chou, and Howell, 2000; Peterson, Myers, and Howell, 1999)—some designed as randomized trials and some not—face challenges because significant percentages of families did not return the year after baseline data were collected, did not fill out all the questionnaire items, or did not complete the standardized tests. A study of a New York City choice program (Barnard, Frangakis, Hill, and Rubin, 2002) featured a design that anticipated these noncompliance issues, and incorporated the use of sophisticated statistical (Bayesian) modeling to estimate the "treatment" effects of the program under these conditions.

A related point is that the U.S. population is a highly mobile one, with people often moving from one geographical area to another, from one home to another, and from one job to another. And their children follow suit, moving among classrooms, schools, districts, and states. According to data collected by the U.S. Census Bureau, 16 percent of the population changed households between March 1999 and March 2000 (Schacter, 2001). This mobility characterizes not only precollege students, but college students as well: nearly one-third of students attend at least two institutions of higher education before completing their undergraduate studies (National Center for Education Statistics, 1996). Students are quite likely to experience different curricula, different teaching methods, and different standards for performance depending on the particular classroom, school or university, district, and state. Thus, researchers engaged in longitudinal research in schools are often faced with substantial shifts in the student population—and thus their study sample—which complicates the tracking of students' learning trajectories over time.

Variability of Educational Programs

Researchers typically must accommodate a rapidly changing reform environment that tends to promote frequent changes in the core education programs a learner encounters. The current education reform movement can be traced back 18 years ago to the report of a Presidential commission, *A Nation at Risk* (National Commission on Excellence in Education, 1983). Since then, the nation has been in a constant process of reforming the schools, and there is no sign that this "tinkering towards utopia" (Tyack and Cuban, 1995) will end soon. Historically, education reform seems to be the norm, not the novelty, in U.S. education, dating back at least to the nineteenth century (Tyack and Cuban, 1995). As one reform idea replaces another, instability in curriculum, standards, and accountability mechanisms is the norm.

Even within reform movements, the state and local control of education significantly shapes the ways that instructional programs and other changes to schooling are implemented, making generalizations difficult. For example, charter schools—public schools that operate under contract with either a state agency or a local school board—take very different forms according to their states' authorizing statutes and the particular contracts (charters) under which the schools operate (RPP International, 2000). While all charter schools are characterized by some degree of flexibility from state education statutes, their educational programming and student populations vary considerably across and within states. The statute that authorizes charter schools in the state of Minnesota, for example, specifically encourages serving children with special needs. By contrast, many (though not all) charter schools in Colorado were founded by well-to-do parents who wanted rigorous academic programs for their children. Consequently, trying to answer a seemingly straightforward question like "Are charter schools more effective in improving student achievement than traditional public schools?" is not particularly useful if one wishes to understand the impact of instructional innovation because the educational environments and programs that fall under the rubric of "charter schools" are so varied that there is no common instructional intervention to evaluate.

Evaluations of changes in curriculum are also influenced by variability in programs. The implementation of curricula is a cyclic process that is governed by a complex mix of state review, teacher input, district leadership, and public comment. Further, new initiatives often require a significant commitment of funds for professional development, which may or may not be available. High stakes accountability systems and national college entrance exams also may complicate the evaluation of the effectiveness of curricular change. Like others we discuss in this chapter, these typical circumstances require that researchers be careful to specify caveats and conditions under which findings are produced.

Organization of Education

Formal schooling takes place in an interdependent, multilayered system. In the preK-12 system, for example, students are assigned to classes, classes are organized by grade level within a school, schools are organized into school districts, school districts may be organized within counties, and counties are subdivisions of states. In addition, within classrooms, students are often placed into different instructional groups based on instructional needs or related issues. And all are influenced by federal education policy. The implication for research is that to understand what is happening at one level, it is often necessary to understand other levels. Thus, a study of how students come to understand key themes in U.S. history, for example, may be influenced by a teacher's approach to history instruction, the value a principal places on history within the curriculum (which influences how much time the teacher has to teach history and the child to learn it), the curriculum adopted by the district (and related decisions to implement the curriculum), and different familial and community factors (e.g., parent and community support of approach to history instruction). In subject areas such as science and mathematics, where accomplishment in later courses is heavily dependent on the quality of early learning, preK-12 school structures can be designed to either facilitate successful remediation or to systematically exclude increasing numbers of students form these courses over time. These differences demand that researchers consider the nature of the vertical organization of the system in their work.

Education researchers have long investigated the interrelationship of these various levels of the system. Statistical methods, for example, can help estimate educational effects on students' history achievement while at the same time accounting for the effects of the multiple layers of the K-12 system (Bryk and Raudenbush, 1988). A study that examined the mechanism by which Catholic schools achieve equitable outcomes for students used such a technique (see Box 5-3).

Diversity

The U.S. population is becoming increasingly diverse in a number of ways, and demographic projections indicate that the trend will continue (Day, 1996). Mirroring the diversity of the broader population, education takes place in specific neighborhoods with their particular geographical, historical, social, ethnic, linguistic, economic, and cultural mixes. For example, students representing dozens of native languages may attend a single school; in some school districts students speak more than 125 languages (Crawford, 1992). This linguistic diversity that characterizes many U.S. schools illustrates the influence of diversity on research. Students from immigrant families are often defined by a characteristic they commonly share—a lack of English fluency. Scratching just below the surface, however, reveals stark differences. Schools serve students who are new immigrants—often unfamiliar with American life beyond what they might have seen in movies—as well as many Hispanics, African Americans, Asian Americans, and American Indians whose families have lived here for generations and who have varying degrees of English proficiency.

Along with linguistic diversity comes diversity in culture, religion, and academic preparation. Some students visit their home country frequently, while others have no contact with their or their parents' birthplaces. Some immigrant students have had excellent schooling in their home countries before coming to the United States; others have had their schooling interrupted by war; and still others have never attended school. Some are illiterate in their own language, and some have languages that were only oral until recently; others come from cultures with long literary traditions. The differences between these students—their age and entry into U.S. schools, the quality of their prior schooling, their native language and the number of native languages represented in their class, their parents' education and English language skills, and their family history and current circumstances—will affect their academic success much more than their common lack of English (Garcia and Wiese, in press). Incorporating such linguistic and sociocultural contexts into the research process is critical to understanding the ways in which these differences influence learning in diverse classrooms.

In sum, the features that shape the application of our principles of science to education research—values and politics, human volition, variability in education programs, the organization of education institutions, and diversity—underscore the important role of context. A specific impli-cation of the role of contextual factors in education research is that the boundaries of generalization from scientific research need to be carefully delineated. Our discussion of diversity above is illustrative: to what extent, for example, is it possible to generalize results of research on suburban middle-class children of Western European descent to inner-city, low-income, limited-English students from Central America or Southeast Asia? Naïve uses and expectations of research that do not recognize such con-textual differences can lead to simplistic, uninformed, and narrow interpre-tations of research and indiscriminate applications. To build theory, formu-late research questions, design and conduct studies, and draw conclusions, scientific education research must attend to such contextual conditions.

This attention to context also suggests that advancing understanding in complex and diverse education settings may require close coordination between researchers and practitioners, interdisciplinary work, and the inter-play between varying forms of education research. It also means a far greater emphasis on taking stock of the inherent diversity of the education experience and its results for different populations of students. In short, it requires specific attention to the contexts of research more frequently and more systematically than has been the case for much of the work in edu-cation to date (National Research Council, 1999c).

FEATURES OF EDUCATION RESEARCH

In addition to the features of education that influence research, there are also aspects of education research as a *field* that help clarify the nature of scientific inquiry in education. A perspective of education research as an enterprise points to some of the infrastructure supports that sustain it, a topic we take up in our consideration of the federal role in supporting education research (Chapter 6). Three of these education research charac-teristics are noteworthy in this regard: its multidisciplinary nature, ethical considerations, and its reliance on relationships with education practitioners.

Multiple Disciplinary Perspectives

The variability and complexity of education are the grist for the academic's disciplinary mill. Multiple scientific disciplines study education and contribute knowledge about it. Economists study the incentive structures of schooling to understand the relationship between interventions designed to change behavior and educational outcomes. Developmental psychologists and subject-matter specialists study fundamental processes of cognition, language, and socialization. Physicists, chemists, and biologists study science curriculum, teaching, and assessment. Organizational sociologists study systems that are organized to meet education goals. Cultural anthropologists study the character and form of social interactions that characterize students' formal and informal educational experiences. Political scientists study the implementation of large-scale institutional change, like charter schools.

The presence of many disciplinary perspectives in education research has at least three implications. First, since several disciplinary perspectives focus on different parts of the system, there are many legitimate research frameworks and methods (Howe and Eisenhart, 1990). But because many disciplines are focusing on different parts of the system, contradictory conclusions may be offered, adding fuel to the debates about both the specific topic and the value of education research. The challenge for the diverse field of education is to integrate theories and empirical findings across domains and methods. Researchers from a range of disciplines working together, therefore, can be particularly valuable. Ongoing work at the Park City Mathematics Institute (see http://www.admin.ias.edu/ma/) provides an example of the potential for interdisciplinary inquiry in education to enhance understanding and promote effective instruction. A diverse group of researchers (from mathematics education, statistics, and psychology) and practitioners (teachers and teacher educators) have joined to conduct research collaboratively on how students understand statistical concepts (e.g., distributions) in order to provide advice to curriculum developers (Jackson, 1996; Day and Kalman, 2001).

A second implication is that advances in education research depend in no small part on advances in related disciplines and fields. Work in the traditional scientific disciplines, as well as in such applied fields as public health may be necessary as infrastructure support for scientific studies in education.

Finally, this proliferation of frameworks, coupled with the sheer scope of the myriad fields that contribute to understanding in education, make the development of professional training for education researchers particularly vexing. The breadth and depth of topical areas as well as multiple epistemological and methodological frameworks are nearly impossible to cover adequately in a single degree program. Conceptualizing how to structure the continuum of professional development for education researchers is similarly challenging, especially since there is little agreement about what scholars in education need to know and be able to do.[1] These unresolved questions have contributed to the uneven preparation of education researchers.

Ethical Considerations

In modern education research, researchers often engage in fieldwork in schools, and with parents, students, and teachers. The need for care and oversight when studying vulnerable populations like children sometimes entails justifiable compromises in the conduct of scientific study and the progress of the scientific enterprise more generally. Ethical issues involving the protection of human participants in research—especially children— have real consequences for the types of designs, data collection, and consequently, results that can be generated from education research.

The need to ensure ethical research conduct may weaken the strength of the research designs that can be used. For example, ethical considerations prohibit withholding education to any student (a common "control" condition in the physical sciences). In studying the effectiveness of an educational program, then, comparisons must almost always be made to standard or existing practice. In this situation, the comparative effect of a new intervention will rarely be large when compared with the standard practice. Also, in some circumstances, researchers may not hide the purposes of a study from the subjects (a common practice in double-blind trials) for ethical reasons.

Ethical issues also have implications for data collection. Parents may refuse to allow their children to participate in a study because of privacy

---

[1]For example, a Spencer Foundation forum aimed at identifying promising mentoring practices in young scholars in education research revealed a number of effective strategies and approaches with no clear patterns (Schoenfeld, 1999).

concerns. Such events can complicate data collection, compromise sampling procedures, and thwart opportunities to generalize. Research ethics requires investigators to design their studies to anticipate these occurrences and to understand and describe their effects on the results of the study.

We briefly consider federal requirements governing research ethics in Chapter 6, where we argue for a federal education research agency to take a leading role in facilitating ethical access to student data.

Relationships

As in other applied fields—such as agriculture, health risk reduction, crime, justice, and welfare—education research relies critically on relationships between researchers and those engaged in professional practice: teachers, administrators, curriculum developers, university deans, school board members, and a host of others. The education research enterprise could not function without these relationships, and its health is correlated strongly with the extent to which these practitioners are willing to participate in or otherwise support research.

Different kinds of research require different levels of participation along a continuum ranging from weak (i.e., short, distant, one-time interaction) to strong (long-term partnership or collaboration). For example, at the weak end of the continuum are research and statistics gathering activities like the National Center for Education Statistics' (NCES) Common Core of Data or the National Assessment of Educational Progress. At the strong end of the continuum lie school reform studies like the one carried out by Bryk and colleagues (Bryk, Sebring, Kerbrow, Rollow, and Easton, 1998) in the Chicago school system. This research is carried out in a collaboration in which district and school personnel have vested interests in the research. Collaborations across disparate parts of universities—between educators and scholars in other disciplines, for example—are another instance of strong relationships that requires careful revision to typical institutional organization. We call these strong relationships partnerships.

Partnerships between researchers and practitioners have become attractive in recent years because the site of much education research has shifted from the laboratory to schools and classrooms (Shulman, 1997). In such field-based work, collaborations with practitioners can bring a form of intellectual capital to the research that cannot be obtained in isolation of practice. Ideally, relationships generate a bidirectional flow to the work, with the research informing practice while craft knowledge and practical wisdom enrich the research. In some cases, important research cannot be conducted without this collaboration. These partnerships are not always easily formed, and often take long periods of time to establish. But they are often essential to develop the trust that is necessary for researchers to perform their jobs adequately and to engage education professionals in a mutually enriching dialogue about the role of research in practice. A current National Research Council effort is attempting to build the capacity of infrastructure for such long-term partnerships to foster research that is useful to practice (see National Research Council, 1999d), and others have suggested that research serve as a basis for long-term communications between researchers and practitioners (Willinsky, 2001). We argue in Chapter 6 that a federal education research agency should help broker such partnerships as part of its investment in strengthening the education research infrastructure.

Another way that some field-based researchers have recently attempted to bring educational practice closer to the research process is by embedding inquiry in "sites of practice" (National Research Council, 2001a). For example, to better understand the knowledge that teachers need to teach third grade mathematics effectively, researchers have grounded their work in concrete examples from teaching practice (e.g., samples of student work solving mathematical problems). Focusing research on these representations of the process of education in practice can generate important insights about the interactive nature of teaching and learning in classrooms (Ball and Lampert, 1999). Engaging in this kind of research, of course, depends on the willingness of school-based practitioners to participate and the establishment of relationships to facilitate it.

As we argue in Chapter 2, with some exceptions, U.S. society has not developed an appetite for using education research as a tool for improving teaching, learning, and schooling (Campbell, 1969). This posture exacerbates the difficulties establishing the relationships necessary to conduct research. The problems with conducting randomized trials attest to this fact: there is little expectation that educational programs or interventions should be subjected to rigorous research (Cook 2001; Burtless, in press). In our own work and in our colleagues', we have found repeatedly that belief and anecdote are often the coin of the realm, and those with commercial interests are not expected by educators, policy makers or the public to use research to support what they sell. We believe that the expectation that research-based information will be available and should be part of the decision-making process needs to be cultivated both in the public and in the research community. With such expectations, it will become increasingly easy to establish the relationships—weak or strong—that are critical for conducting education research. Simply put, researchers need practitioners and practitioners need researchers. Without these relationships, a great deal of scientific research in education is likely to be piecemeal and opportunistic, and educators are unlikely to draw on scientific knowledge to improve their practices in any meaningful way.

This chapter provides a flavor for the particular character of scientific inquiry in education. We elaborate how the guiding principles and features of education are united within a variety of study designs in the next chapter, where we discuss, and provide examples of, how education researchers approach particular types of inquiries.

5

Designs for the Conduct of Scientific Research in Education

The salient features of education delineated in Chapter 4 and the guiding principles of scientific research laid out in Chapter 3 set boundaries for the design and conduct of scientific education research. Thus, the design of a study (e.g., randomized experiment, ethnography, multiwave survey) does not itself make it scientific. However, if the design directly addresses a question that can be addressed empirically, is linked to prior research and relevant theory, is competently implemented in context, logically links the findings to interpretation ruling out counterinterpretations, and is made accessible to scientific scrutiny, it could then be considered scientific. That is: Is there a clear set of questions underlying the design? Are the methods appropriate to answer the questions and rule out competing answers? Does the study take previous research into account? Is there a conceptual basis? Are data collected in light of local conditions and analyzed systematically? Is the study clearly described and made available for criticism? The more closely aligned it is with these principles, the higher the quality of the scientific study. And the particular features of education require that the research process be explicitly designed to anticipate the implications of these features and to model and plan accordingly.

RESEARCH DESIGN

Our scientific principles include research design—the subject of this chapter—as but one aspect of a larger process of rigorous inquiry. However, research design (and corresponding scientific methods) is a crucial aspect of science. It is also the subject of much debate in many fields, including education. In this chapter, we describe some of the most frequently used and trusted designs for scientifically addressing broad classes of research questions in education.

In doing so, we develop three related themes. First, as we posit earlier, a variety of legitimate scientific approaches exist in education research. Therefore, the description of methods discussed in this chapter is illustrative of a range of trusted approaches; it should not be taken as an authoritative list of tools to the exclusion of any others.[1] As we stress in earlier chapters, the history of science has shown that research designs evolve, as do the questions they address, the theories they inform, and the overall state of knowledge.

Second, we extend the argument we make in Chapter 3 that designs and methods must be carefully selected and implemented to best address the question at hand. Some methods are better than others for particular purposes, and scientific inferences are constrained by the type of design employed. Methods that may be appropriate for estimating the effect of an educational intervention, for example, would rarely be appropriate for use in estimating dropout rates. While researchers—in education or any other field—may overstate the conclusions from an inquiry, the strength of scientific inference must be judged in terms of the design used to address the question under investigation. A comprehensive explication of a hierarchy of appropriate designs and analytic approaches under various conditions would require a depth of treatment found in research methods textbooks. This is not our objective. Rather, our goal is to illustrate that among available techniques, certain designs are better suited to address particular kinds of questions under particular conditions than others.

Third, in order to generate a rich source of scientific knowledge in education that is refined and revised over time, different types of inquiries and methods are required. At any time, the types of questions and methods depend in large part on an accurate assessment of the overall state of knowl-

---

[1]Numerous textbooks and treatments map the domain of design (e.g., Kelly and Lesh, 2000) for the various types of inquiries in education. We refer to several of the seminal works on research methodology throughout the chapter.

edge and professional judgment about how a particular line of inquiry could advance understanding. In areas with little prior knowledge, for example, research will generally need to involve careful description to formulate initial ideas. In such situations, descriptive studies might be undertaken to help bring education problems or trends into sharper relief or to generate plausible theories about the underlying structure of behavior or learning. If the effects of education programs that have been implemented on a large scale are to be understood, however, investigations must be designed to test a set of causal hypotheses. Thus, while we treat the topic of design in this chapter as applying to individual studies, research design has a broader quality as it relates to lines of inquiry that develop over time.

While a full development of these notions goes considerably beyond our charge, we offer this brief overview to place the discussion of methods that follows into perspective. Also, in the concluding section of this chapter, we make a few targeted suggestions for the kinds of work we believe are most needed in education research to make further progress toward robust knowledge.

TYPES OF RESEARCH QUESTIONS

In discussing design, we have to be true to our admonition that the research question drives the design, not vice versa. To simplify matters, the committee recognized that a great number of education research questions fall into three (interrelated) types: description—What is happening? cause—Is there a systematic effect? and process or mechanism—Why or how is it happening?

The first question—What is happening?—invites description of various kinds, so as to properly characterize a population of students, understand the scope and severity of a problem, develop a theory or conjecture, or identify changes over time among different educational indicators—for example, achievement, spending, or teacher qualifications. Description also can include associations among variables, such as the characteristics of schools (e.g., size, location, economic base) that are related to (say) the provision of music and art instruction. The second question is focused on establishing causal effects: Does x cause y? The search for cause, for example, can include seeking to understand the effect of teaching strategies on student learning or state policy changes on district resource decisions. The third question confronts the need to understand the mechanism or process by which x causes y. Studies that seek to model how various parts of a complex system—like U.S. education—fit together help explain the conditions that facilitate or impede change in teaching, learning, and schooling. Within each type of question, we separate the discussion into subsections that show the use of different methods given more fine-grained goals and conditions of an inquiry.

Although for ease of discussion we treat these types of questions separately, in practice they are closely related. As our examples show, within particular studies, several kinds of queries can be addressed. Furthermore, various genres of scientific education research often address more than one of these types of questions. Evaluation research—the rigorous and systematic evaluation of an education program or policy—exemplifies the use of multiple questions and corresponding designs. As applied in education, this type of scientific research is distinguished from other scientific research by its purpose: to contribute to program improvement (Weiss, 1998a). Evaluation often entails an assessment of whether the program caused improvements in the outcome or outcomes of interest (Is there a systematic effect?). It also can involve detailed descriptions of the way the program is implemented in practice and in what contexts (What is happening?) and the ways that program services influence outcomes (How is it happening?).

Throughout the discussion, we provide several examples of scientific education research, connecting them to scientific principles (Chapter 3) and the features of education (Chapter 4). We have chosen these studies because they align closely with several of the scientific principles. These examples include studies that generate hypotheses or conjectures as well as those that test them. Both tasks are essential to science, but as a general rule they cannot be accomplished simultaneously.

Moreover, just as we argue that the design of a study does not itself make it scientific, an investigation that seeks to address one of these questions is not necessarily scientific either. For example, many descriptive studies—however useful they may be—bear little resemblance to careful scientific study. They might record observations without any clear conceptual viewpoint, without reproducible protocols for recording data, and so forth. Again, studies may be considered scientific by assessing the rigor with which they meet scientific principles and are designed to account for the context of the study.

Finally, we have tended to speak of research in terms of a simple dichotomy— scientific or not scientific—but the reality is more complicated. Individual research projects may adhere to each of the principles in varying degrees, and the extent to which they meet these goals goes a long way toward defining the scientific quality of a study. For example, while all scientific studies must pose clear questions that can be investigated empirically and be grounded in existing knowledge, more rigorous studies will begin with more precise statements of the underlying theory driving the inquiry and will generally have a well-specified hypothesis before the data collection and testing phase is begun. Studies that do not start with clear conceptual frameworks and hypotheses may still be scientific, although they are obviously at a more rudimentary level and will generally require follow-on study to contribute significantly to scientific knowledge.

Similarly, lines of research encompassing collections of studies may be more or less productive and useful in advancing knowledge. An area of research that, for example, does not advance beyond the descriptive phase toward more precise scientific investigation of causal effects and mechanisms for a long period of time is clearly not contributing as much to knowledge as one that builds on prior work and moves toward more complete understanding of the causal structure. This is not to say that descriptive work cannot generate important breakthroughs. However, the rate of progress should—as we discuss at the end of this chapter—enter into consideration of the support for advanced lines of inquiry. The three classes of questions we discuss in the remainder of this chapter are ordered in a way that reflects the sequence that research studies tend to follow as well as their interconnected nature.

WHAT IS HAPPENING?

Answers to "What is happening?" questions can be found by following Yogi Berra's counsel in a systematic way: if you want to know what's going on, you have to go out and look at what is going on. Such inquiries are descriptive. They are intended to provide a range of information from documenting trends and issues in a range of geopolitical jurisdictions, populations, and institutions to rich descriptions of the complexities of educational practice in a particular locality, to relationships among such elements as socioeconomic status, teacher qualifications, and achievement.

Estimates of Population Characteristics

Descriptive scientific research in education can make generalizable statements about the national scope of a problem, student achievement levels across the states, or the demographics of children, teachers, or schools. Methods that enable the collection of data from a randomly selected sample of the population provide the best way of addressing such questions. Questionnaires and telephone interviews are common survey instruments developed to gather information from a representative sample of some population of interest. Policy makers at the national, state, and sometimes district levels depend on this method to paint a picture of the educational landscape. Aggregate estimates of the academic achievement level of children at the national level (e.g., National Center for Education Statistics [NCES], National Assessment of Educational Progress [NAEP]), the supply, demand, and turnover of teachers (e.g., NCES Schools and Staffing Survey), the nation's dropout rates (e.g., NCES Common Core of Data), how U.S. children fare on tests of mathematics and science achievement relative to children in other nations (e.g., Third International Mathematics and Science Study) and the distribution of doctorate degrees across the nation (e.g., National Science Foundation's Science and Engineering Indicators) are all based on surveys from populations of school children, teachers, and schools.

To yield credible results, such data collection usually depends on a random sample (alternatively called a probability sample) of the target population. If every observation (e.g., person, school) has a known chance of being selected into the study, researchers can make estimates of the larger population of interest based on statistical technology and theory. The validity of inferences about population characteristics based on sample data depends heavily on response rates, that is, the percentage of those randomly selected for whom data are collected. The measures used must have known reliability—that is, the extent to which they reproduce results. Finally, the value of a data collection instrument hinges not only on the sampling method, participation rate, and reliability, but also on their validity: that the questionnaire or survey items measure what they are supposed to measure.

The NAEP survey tracks national trends in student achievement across several subject domains and collects a range of data on school, student, and teacher characteristics (see Box 5-1). This rich source of information enables several kinds of descriptive work. For example, researchers can estimate the average score of eighth graders on the mathematics assessment (i.e., measures of central tendency) and compare that performance to prior years. Part of the study we feature (see below) about college women's career choices featured a similar estimation of population characteristics. In that study, the researchers developed a survey to collect data from a representative sample of women at the two universities to aid them in assessing the generalizability of their findings from the in-depth studies of the 23 women.

Simple Relationships

The NAEP survey also illustrates how researchers can describe patterns of relationships between variables. For example, NCES reports that in 2000, eighth graders whose teachers majored in mathematics or mathematics education scored higher, on average, than did students whose teachers did not major in these fields (U.S. Department of Education, 2000). This finding is the result of descriptive work that explores the correlation between variables: in this case, the relationship between student mathematics performance and their teachers' undergraduate major.

Such associations cannot be used to infer cause. However, there is a common tendency to make unsubstantiated jumps from establishing a relationship to concluding cause. As committee member Paul Holland quipped during the committee's deliberations, "Casual comparisons inevitably invite careless causal conclusions." To illustrate the problem with drawing causal inferences from simple correlations, we use an example from work that compares Catholic schools to public schools. We feature this study later in the chapter as one that competently examines causal mechanisms. Before addressing questions of mechanism, foundational work involved simple correlational results that compared the performance of Catholic high school students on standardized mathematics tests with their

BOX 5-1
National Assessment of Educational Progress

Simply collecting data is not in and of itself scientific. It is the rigorous organization and analysis of data to answer clearly specified questions that form the basis of scientific description, not the data themselves. Quantitative data appear in many ways in education research; their most common form of organization is as a "units-by-variables" array. The National Assessment of Educational Progress (NAEP) is an instructive example. This large survey (implemented and maintained by the National Center for Education Statistics) of 4th, 8th, and 12th graders in the United States collects information on a variety of academic subject areas, including mathematics and literacy, from samples drawn from these grades on a regular schedule.

There are several types of units*, for example, students and teachers. Information is systematically collected from both students and teachers in areas that are appropriate to each type of unit. For students, NAEP collects data on academic performance as well as background information. Teachers are surveyed about their training and experience and their methods of instruction. The units-by-variables organization of data is important because each row corresponds to all the data for each unit and the columns correspond to the information represented by a single variable across all the units in the study. Modern psychometric methods are available to summarize this complex set of information into reports on student achievement and its relation to other factors. This combination of rigorous data collection, analysis, and reporting is what distinguishes scientific description from casual observation.

---

*"Unit" is strictly a technical term that refers to the class or type of phenomena being studied, such as student, teacher, or state.

counterparts in public schools. These simple correlations revealed that average mathematics achievement was considerably higher for Catholic school students than for public school students (Bryk, Lee, and Holland, 1993). However, the researchers were careful *not* to conclude from this analysis that attending a Catholic school *causes* better student outcomes, because there are a host of potential explanations (other than attending a Catholic school) for this relationship between school type and achievement. For example, since Catholic schools can screen children for aptitude, they may have a more able student population than public schools at the outset. (This is an example of the classic selectivity bias that commonly threatens the validity of causal claims in nonrandomized studies; we return to this issue in the next section.) In short, there are other hypotheses that could explain the observed differences in achievement between students in different sectors that must be considered systematically in assessing the potential causal relationship between Catholic schooling and student outcomes.

Descriptions of Localized Educational Settings

In some cases, scientists are interested in the fine details (rather than the distribution or central tendency) of what is happening in a particular organization, group of people, or setting. This type of work is especially important when good information about the group or setting is non-existent or scant. In this type of research, then, it is important to obtain first-hand, in-depth information from the particular focal group or site. For such purposes, selecting a random sample from the population of interest may not be the proper method of choice; rather, samples may be purposively selected to illuminate phenomena in depth.[2] For example, to better understand a high-achieving school in an urban setting with children of predominantly low socioeconomic status, a researcher might conduct a detailed case study or an ethnographic study (a case study with a focus on culture) of such a school (Yin and White, 1986; Miles and Huberman,

---

[2]This is not to say that probability sampling is always irrelevant with respect to case studies. A collection of case studies selected randomly from a population may be developed.

1994). This type of scientific description can provide rich depictions of the policies, procedures, and contexts in which the school operates and generate plausible hypotheses about what might account for its success. Researchers often spend long periods of time in the setting or group in order to understand what decisions are made, what beliefs and attitudes are formed, what relationships are developed, and what forms of success are celebrated. These descriptions, when used in conjunction with causal methods, are often critical to understand such educational outcomes as student achievement because they illuminate key contextual factors.

Box 5-2 provides an example of a study that described in detail (and also modeled several possible mechanisms; see later discussion) a small group of women, half who began their college careers in science and half in what were considered more traditional majors for women. This descriptive part of the inquiry involved an ethnographic study of the lives of 23 first-year women enrolled in two large universities.

Scientific description of this type can generate systematic observations about the focal group or site, and patterns in results may be generalizable to other similar groups or sites or for the future. As with any other method, a scientifically rigorous case study has to be designed to address the research question it addresses. That is, the investigator has to choose sites, occasions, respondents, and times with a clear research purpose in mind and be sensitive to his or her own expectations and biases (Maxwell, 1996; Silverman, 1993). Data should typically be collected from varied sources, by varied methods, and corroborated by other investigators. Furthermore, the account of the case needs to draw on original evidence and provide enough detail so that the reader can make judgments about the validity of the conclusions (Yin, 2000).

Results may also be used as the basis for new theoretical developments, new experiments, or improved measures on surveys that indicate the extent of generalizability. In the work done by Holland and Eisenhart (1990), for example (see Box 5-2), a number of theoretical models were developed and tested to explain how women decide to pursue or abandon nontraditional careers in the fields they had studied in college. Their finding that commitment to college life—not fear of competing with men or other hypotheses that had previously been set forth—best explained these decisions was new knowledge. It has been shown in subsequent studies to

BOX 5-2
College Women's Career Choices

In the late 1970s cultural anthropologists Dorothy Holland and Margaret Eisenhart set out to learn more about why so few women who began their college careers in nontraditional majors (e.g., science, mathematics, computer science) ended up working in those fields. At the time, several different explanations were being proposed: Women were not well prepared before coming to college; women were discriminated against in college; women did not want to compete with men for jobs. Holland and Eisenhart (1990) first designed ethnographic case studies of a small group of freshman women at two public, residential universities—one historically black, one historically white. From volunteers on each campus, matched groups were selected—based on a survey of their high school grades, college majors, college activities, and college peers. All of the 23 women who participated had at least a B+ average in high school. Half from each campus were planning traditional majors for women; half were planning nontraditional majors.

Based on analysis of the ethnographic data obtained from a year of participant observation and open-ended interviews with the women, models were developed to describe how the 23 women participated in college life. The models depicted three different kinds of commitment to school work in college. Each model included: (1) the women's views about the value of schoolwork; (2) their reasons for doing schoolwork; (3) and the perceived costs (both financial and social) of doing schoolwork. Extrapolating from the models, the researchers predicted what each woman would do after college—continue in school, get a job in her field, get a job outside of her field, get married, etc. At the end of 4 years and again after 3 more years, the researchers followed up with telephone interviews with each woman. In *all* 23 cases, their predictions made based on the models of commitment to schoolwork were confirmed. Also, in all cases, the models of commitment were better predictors of the future than precollege preparation (grades, courses taken), discrimination against women, or feelings about competing with men.

generalize somewhat to similar schools, though additional models seem to exist at some schools (Seymour and Hewitt, 1997).

Although such purposively selected samples may not be scientifically generalizable to other locations or people, these vivid descriptions often appeal to practitioners. Scientifically rigorous case studies have strengths and weaknesses for such use. They can, for example, help local decision makers by providing them with ideas and strategies that have promise in their educational setting. They cannot (unless combined with other methods) provide estimates of the likelihood that an educational approach might work under other conditions or that they have identified the right underlying causes. As we argue throughout this volume, research designs can often be strengthened considerably by using multiple methods—integrating the use of both quantitative estimates of population characteristics and qualitative studies of localized context.

Other descriptive designs may involve interviews with respondents or document reviews in a fairly large number of cases, such as 30 school districts or 60 colleges. Cases are often selected to represent a variety of conditions (e.g., urban/rural; east/west; affluent/poor). Such descriptive studies can be longitudinal, returning to the same cases over several years to see how conditions change.

These examples of descriptive work meet the principles of science, and have clearly contributed important insights to the base of scientific knowledge. If research is to be used to answer questions about "what works," however, it must advance to other levels of scientific investigation such as those considered next.

IS THERE A SYSTEMATIC EFFECT?

Research designs that attempt to identify systematic effects have at their root an intent to establish a cause-and-effect relationship. Causal work is built on both theory and descriptive studies. In other words, the search for causal effects cannot be conducted in a vacuum: ideally, a strong theoretical base as well as extensive descriptive information are in place to provide the intellectual foundation for understanding causal relationships.

The simple question of "does x cause y?" typically involves several different kinds of studies undertaken sequentially (Holland, 1993). In basic terms, several conditions must be met to establish cause. Usually, a relationship or correlation between the variables is first identified.[3] Researchers also confirm that x preceded y in time (temporal sequence) and, crucially, that all presently conceivable rival explanations for the observed relationship have been "ruled out." As alternative explanations are eliminated, confidence increases that it was indeed x that caused y. "Ruling out" competing explanations is a central metaphor in medical research, diagnosis, and other fields, including education, and it is the key element of causal queries (Campbell and Stanley 1963; Cook and Campbell 1979, 1986).

The use of multiple qualitative methods, especially in conjunction with a comparative study of the kind we describe in this section, can be particularly helpful in ruling out alternative explanations for the results observed (Yin, 2000; Weiss, in press). Such investigative tools can enable stronger causal inferences by enhancing the analysis of whether competing explanations can account for patterns in the data (e.g., unreliable measures or contamination of the comparison group). Similarly, qualitative methods can examine possible explanations for observed effects that arise outside of the purview of the study. For example, while an intervention was in progress, another program or policy may have offered participants opportunities similar to, and reinforcing of, those that the intervention provided. Thus, the "effects" that the study observed may have been due to the other program ("history" as the counterinterpretation; see Chapter 3). When all plausible rival explanations are identified and various forms of data can be used as evidence to rule them out, the causal claim that the intervention caused the observed effects is strengthened. In education, research that explores students' and teachers' in-depth experiences, observes their actions, and documents the constraints that affect their day-to-day activities provides a key source of generating plausible causal hypotheses.

We have organized the remainder of this section into two parts. The first treats randomized field trials, an ideal method when entities being examined can be randomly assigned to groups. Experiments are especially well-suited to situations in which the causal hypothesis is relatively simple. The second describes situations in which randomized field trials are not

---

[3]In some cases, a simple correlation between two variables may not exist when a cause-effect relationship does because of the counterbalancing effect of related factors.

feasible or desirable, and showcases a study that employed causal modeling techniques to address a complex causal question. We have distinguished randomized studies from others primarily to signal the difference in the strength with which causal claims can typically be made from them. The key difference between randomized field trials and other methods with respect to making causal claims is the extent to which the assumptions that underlie them are testable. By this simple criterion, nonrandomized studies are weaker in their ability to establish causation than randomized field trials, in large part because the role of other factors in influencing the outcome of interest is more difficult to gauge in nonrandomized studies. Other conditions that affect the choice of method are discussed in the course of the section.

Causal Relationships When Randomization Is Feasible

A fundamental scientific concept in making causal claims—that is, inferring that x caused y—is comparison. Comparing outcomes (e.g., student achievement) between two groups that are similar except for the causal variable (e.g., the educational intervention) helps to isolate the effect of that causal agent on the outcome of interest.[4] As we discuss in Chapter 4, it is sometimes difficult to retain the sharpness of a comparison in education due to proximity (e.g., a design that features students in one classroom assigned to different interventions is subject to "spillover" effects) or human volition (e.g., teacher, parent, or student decisions to switch to another condition threaten the integrity of the randomly formed groups). Yet, from a scientific perspective, randomized trials (we also use the term "experiment" to refer to causal studies that feature random assignment) are the ideal for establishing whether one or more factors caused change in an outcome because of their strong ability to enable fair comparisons (Campbell and Stanley, 1963; Boruch, 1997; Cook and Payne, in press). Random allocation of students, classrooms, schools—whatever the unit of comparison may be—to different treatment groups assures that these comparison groups are, roughly speaking, equivalent at the time an intervention is introduced (that is, they do not differ systematically on account of hidden

---

[4]Specifically, using comparison groups helps illuminate the "counterfactual," or what would have happened under different circumstances.

influences) and chance differences between the groups can be taken into account statistically. As a result, the independent effect of the intervention on the outcome of interest can be isolated. In addition, these studies enable legitimate statistical statements of confidence in the results.

The Tennessee STAR experiment (see Chapter 3) on class-size reduction is a good example of the use of randomization to assess cause in an education study; in particular, this tool was used to gauge the effectiveness of an intervention. Some policy makers and scientists were unwilling to accept earlier, largely nonexperimental studies on class-size reduction as a basis for major policy decisions in the state. Those studies could not guarantee a fair comparison of children in small versus large classes because the comparisons relied on statistical adjustment rather than on actual construction of statistically equivalent groups. In Tennessee, statistical equivalence was achieved by randomly assigning eligible children and teachers to classrooms of different size. If the trial was properly carried out,[5] this randomization would lead to an unbiased estimate of the relative effect of class-size reduction and a statistical statement of confidence in the results.

Randomized trials are used frequently in the medical sciences and certain areas of the behavioral and social sciences, including prevention studies of mental health disorders (e.g., Beardslee, Wright, Salt, and Drezner, 1997), behavioral approaches to smoking cessation (e.g., Pieterse, Seydel, DeVries, Mudde, and Kok, 2001), and drug abuse prevention (e.g., Cook, Lawrence, Morse, and Roehl, 1984). It would not be ethical to assign individuals randomly to smoke and drink, and thus much of the evidence regarding the harmful effects of nicotine and alcohol comes from descriptive and correlational studies. However, randomized trials that show reductions in health detriments and improved social and behavioral functioning strengthen the causal links that have been established between drug use and adverse health and behavioral outcomes (Moses, 1995; Mosteller, Gilbert, and McPeek, 1980). In medical research, the relative effectiveness of the Salk vaccine (see Lambert and Markel, 2000) and streptomycin (Medical Research Council, 1948) was demonstrated through such trials. We have also learned about which drugs and surgical treatments are useless by depending on randomized controlled experiments (e.g., Schulte et al.,

---

[5]We make this caveat to acknowledge debate in the field about whether the randomized field trial in the Tennessee study was implemented properly.

2001; Gorman et al., 2001; Paradise et al., 1999). Randomized controlled trials are also used in industrial, market, and agricultural research.

Such trials are not frequently conducted in education research (Boruch, De Moya, and Snyder, in press). Nonetheless, it is not difficult to identify good examples in a variety of education areas that demonstrate their feasibility (see Boruch, 1997; Orr, 1999; and Cook and Payne, in press). For example, among the education programs whose effectiveness have been evaluated in randomized trials are the *Sesame Street* television series (Bogatz and Ball, 1972), peer-assisted learning and tutoring for young children with reading problems (Fuchs, Fuchs, and Kazdan, 1999), and Upward Bound (Myers and Schirm, 1999). And many of these trials have been successfully implemented on a large scale, randomizing entire classrooms or schools to intervention conditions. For numerous examples of trials in which schools, work places, and other entities are the units of random allocation and analysis, see Murray (1998), Donner and Klar (2000), Boruch and Foley (2000), and the Campbell Collaboration register of trials at http://campbell.gse.upenn.edu.

Causal Relationships When Randomization Is Not Feasible

In this section we discuss the conditions under which randomization is not feasible nor desirable, highlight alternative methods for addressing causal questions, and provide an illustrative example. Many nonexperimental methods and analytic approaches are commonly classified under the blanket rubric "quasi-experiment" because they attempt to approximate the underlying logic of the experiment without random assignment (Campbell and Stanley, 1963; Caporaso and Roos, 1973). These designs were developed because social science researchers recognized that in some social contexts (e.g., schools), researchers do not have the control afforded in laboratory settings and thus cannot always randomly assign units (e.g., classrooms).

Quasi-experiments (alternatively called observational studies),[6] for example, sometimes compare groups of interest that exist naturally (e.g.,

---

[6]The terms "quasi-experiment" and "observational study" are not equivalent, but for our purposes are essentially interchangeable. For finer distinctions, see Cochran (1983) and Rosenbaum (1995) on observational studies and Cook and Campbell (1986) on quasi-experiments.

existing classes varying in size) rather than assigning them randomly to different conditions (e.g., assigning students to small, medium, or large class size). These studies must attempt to ensure fair comparisons through means other than randomization, such as by using statistical techniques to adjust for background variables that may account for differences in the outcome of interest. For example, researchers might come across schools that vary in the size of their classes and compare the achievement of students in large and small classes, adjusting for other differences among schools and children. If the class size conjecture holds after this adjustment is made, the researchers would expect students in smaller classes to have higher achievement scores than students in larger size classes. If indeed this difference is observed, the causal effect is more plausible.

The plausibility of the researchers' causal interpretation, however, depends on some strong assumptions. They must assume that their attempts to equate schools and children were, indeed, successful. Yet, there is always the possibility that some unmeasured, prior existing difference among schools and children caused the effect, not the reduced class size. Or, there is the possibility that teachers with reduced classes were actively involved in school reform and that their increased effort and motivation (which might wane over time) caused the effect, not the smaller classes themselves. In short, these designs are less effective at eliminating competing plausible hypotheses with the same authority as a true experiment.

The major weakness of nonrandomized designs is selectivity bias—the counter-interpretation that the treatment did not cause the difference in outcomes but, rather, unmeasured prior existing differences (differential selectivity) between the groups did.[7] For example, a comparison of early literacy skills among low-income children who participated in a local preschool program and those who did not may be confounded by selectivity bias. That is, the parents of the children who were enrolled in preschool may be more motivated than other parents to provide reading experiences to their children at home, thus making it difficult to disentangle the several potential causes (e.g., preschool program or home reading experiences) for early reading success.

---

[7]Classic treatments of selection bias and other common "threats to internal validity" can be found in texts from many different disciplines: see for example, Campbell (1957); Heckman (2001); and Denzin (1978).

It is critical in such studies, then, to be aware of potential sources of bias and to measure them so their influence can be accounted for in relation to the outcome of interest.[8] It is when these biases are not known that quasi-experiments may yield misleading results. Thus, the scientific principle of making assumptions explicit and carefully attending to ruling out competing hypotheses about what caused a difference takes on heightened importance.

In some settings, well-controlled quasi-experiments may have greater "external validity"—generalizability to other people, times, and settings— than experiments with completely random assignment (Cronbach et al., 1980; Weiss, 1998a). It may be useful to take advantage of the experience and investment of a school with a particular program and try to design a quasi-experiment that compares the school that has a good implementation of the program to a similar school without the program (or with a different program). In such cases, there is less risk of poor implementation, more investment of the implementers in the program, and potentially greater impact. The findings may be more generalizable than in a randomized experiment because the latter may be externally mandated (i.e., by the researcher) and thus may not be feasible to implement in the "real-life" practice of education settings. The results may also have stronger external validity because if a school or district uses a single program, the possible contamination of different programs because teachers or administrators talk and interact will be reduced. Random assignment within a school at the level of the classroom or child often carries the risk of dilution or blending the programs. If assignment is truly random, such threats to internal validity will not bias the comparison of programs—just the estimation of the strength of the effects.

In the section above (What Is Happening?), we note that some kinds of correlational work make important contributions to understanding broad patterns of relationships among educational phenomena; here, we highlight a correlational design that allows causal inferences about the relationship between two or more variables. When correlational methods use what are called "model-fitting" techniques based on a theoretically gener-

---

[8]Recent methodological advances—instrumental variables in particular—attempt to address the problem of selection in nonrandomized causal studies. The study described in Box 5-3 utilized this technique.

ated system of variables, they permit stronger, albeit still tentative, causal inferences.

In Chapter 3, we offer an example that illustrates the use of model-fitting techniques from the geophysical sciences that tested alternative hypotheses about the causes of glaciation. In Box 5-3, we provide an example of causal modeling that shows the value of such techniques in education. This work examined the potential causal connection between teacher compensation and student dropout rates. Exploring this relationship is quite relevant to education policy, but it cannot be studied through a randomized field trail: teacher salaries, of course, cannot be randomly assigned nor can students be randomly assigned to those teachers. Because important questions like these often cannot be examined experimentally, statisticians have developed sophisticated model-fitting techniques to statistically rule out potential alternative explanations and deal with the problem of selection bias.

The key difference between simple correlational work and model-fitting is that the latter enhances causal attribution. In the study examining teacher compensation and dropout rates, for example, researchers introduced a conceptual model for the relationship between student outcomes and teacher salary, set forth an explicit hypothesis to test about the nature of that relationship, and assessed competing models of interpretation. By empirically rejecting competing theoretical models, confidence is increased in the explanatory power of the remaining model(s) (although other alternative models may also exist that provide a comparable fit to the data).

The study highlighted in Box 5-3 tested different models in this way. Loeb and Page (2000) took a fresh look at a question that had a good bit of history, addressing what appeared to be converging evidence that there was no causal relationship between teacher salaries and student outcomes. They reasoned that one possible explanation for these results was that the usual "production-function" model for the effects of salary on student outcomes was inadequately specified. Specifically, they hypothesized that nonpecuniary job characteristics and alternative wage opportunities that previous models had not accounted for may be relevant in understanding the relationship between teacher compensation and student outcomes. After incorporating these opportunity costs in their model and finding a sophisticated way to control the fact that wealthier parents are likely to send their

BOX 5-3
Teacher Salaries and Student Outcomes

In several comprehensive reviews of research on the effects of educational expenditures on student outcomes, Hanushek (1986, 1997) found that student outcomes were not consistently related either to per-pupil outlays or to teacher salaries. Grogger (1996), Betts (1995), and Altonji (1988), using national longitudinal data sets, produced similar results.

However, Loeb and Page (2000) noted a discrepancy between these findings and studies that found school and non-salary teacher effects (e.g., Altonji, 1988; Ehrenberg and Brewer, 1994; Ferguson, 1991). Indeed, Hanushek, Kain, and Rivkin (1998) found a reliable relationship between teacher quality and students' achievement. For Loeb and Page, these findings add a new dimension to the puzzle. "If teacher quality affects student achievement, then why do studies that predict student outcomes from teacher wages produce weak results?" (2000, p. 393).

Loeb and Page pointed out that the previous education expenditure studies failed to account for nonmonetary job characteristics and opportunities that might be open to would-be teachers in the local job market ("opportunity costs"). Both might affect a qualified teacher's decision to teach. Consequently, they tested two competing models, the commonly used "production function" model, which predicted outcomes from expenditures and had formed the theoretical basis of most prior work on the topic, and a modified production-function model that incorporated opportunity costs. They replicated prior findings using traditional production-function procedures from previous studies. However, once they statistically adjusted for opportunity costs, they found that raising teacher wages by 10 percent reduced high school dropout rates by 3-4 percent. They suggested that previous research on the effects of teacher wages on student outcomes failed to show effects because they lacked adequate controls for nonwage aspects of teaching and market differences in alternative occupational opportunities.

children to schools that pay teachers more, Loeb and Page found that raising teacher wages by 10 percent reduced high school dropout rates by 3 to 4 percent.

WHY OR HOW IS IT HAPPENING?

In many situations, finding that a causal agent (x) leads to the outcome (y) is not sufficient. Important questions remain about *how x* causes *y*. Questions about how things work demand attention to the processes and mechanisms by which the causes produce their effects. However, scientific research can also legitimately proceed in the opposite direction: that is, the search for mechanism can come before an effect has been established. For example, if the process by which an intervention influences student outcomes is established, researchers can often predict its effectiveness with known probability. In either case, the processes and mechanisms should be linked to theories so as to form an explanation for the phenomena of interest.

The search for causal mechanisms, especially once a causal effect has garnered strong empirical support, can use all of the designs we have discussed. In Chapter 2, we trace a sequence of investigations in molecular biology that investigated how genes are turned on and off. Very different techniques, but ones that share the same basic intellectual approach to casual analysis reflected in these genetic studies, have yielded understandings in education. Consider, for example, the Tennessee class-size experiment (see discussion in Chapter 3). In addition to examining whether reduced class size produced achievement benefits, especially for minority students, a research team and others in the field asked (see, e.g., Grissmer, 1999) what might explain the Tennessee and other class-size effects. That is, what was the causal mechanism through which reduced class size affected achievement? To this end, researchers (Bohrnstedt and Stecher, 1999) used classroom observations and interviews to compare teaching in different class sizes. They conducted ethnographic studies in search of mechanism. They correlated measures of teaching behavior with student achievement scores. These questions are important because they enhance understanding of the foundational processes at work when class size is reduced and thus improve the capacity to implement these reforms effectively in different times, places, and contexts.

Exploring Mechanism When Theory Is Fairly Well Established

A well-known study of Catholic schools provides another example of a rigorous attempt to understand mechanism (see Box 5-4). Previous and highly controversial work on Catholic schools (e.g., Coleman, Hoffer, and

---

BOX 5-4
Effective Schooling: A Comparison of Catholic Schools and Public Schools

In the early 1980s two influential books (Coleman, Hoffer, and Kilgore, 1982; Greeley, 1982) set off years of controversy and debate in academic and policy circles about the relative effectiveness of Catholic schools and public schools. In a synthesis of several lines of inquiry over a 10-year period, Bryk and colleagues (Byrk, Lee, and Holland, 1993) focused attention on *how* Catholic schools functioned to better understand this prior work and to offer insights about improving schools more generally. This longitudinal study is an excellent example of the use of multiple methods, both quantitative and qualitative, to generate converging evidence about such a complex topic. It featured in-depth case studies of seven particularly successful Catholic schools, descriptive profiles of Catholic schools nationally, and sophisticated statistical modeling techniques to assess causal mechanism.

One line of inquiry within this multilayered study featured a quasi-experiment that compared the mathematics achievement of Catholic high school students and public high school students. Using simple correlational techniques, the researchers showed that the social distribution of academic achievement was more equalized in Catholic than non-Catholic schools: for

---

Kilgore, 1982) had examined the relative benefits to students of Catholic and public schools. Drawing on these studies, as well as a fairly substantial literature related to effective schools, Bryk and his colleagues (Byrk, Lee, and Holland, 1993) focused on the mechanism by which Catholic schools seemed to achieve success relative to public schools. A series of models were developed (sector effects only, compositional effects, and school effects) and tested to explain the mechanism by which Catholic schools successfully achieve an equitable social distribution of academic achievement. The

example, the achievement gap between minority and non-minority students was smaller in Catholic schools than in public schools. To better understand the possible causes behind these "sector" differences, Bryk and his colleagues used data from a rich, longitudinal data set to test whether certain features of school organization explained these differences and predicted success. Because students in this data set were not randomly assigned to attend Catholic or public schools, the researchers attempted to ensure fair comparisons by statistically holding constant other variables (such as student background) that could also explain the finding about the social distribution of achievement. Three potential explanatory models were developed and tested with respect to explaining the relative effectiveness of Catholic schools: sector effects only (the private and spiritual nature of Catholic schools); compositional effects (the composition of the student body in Catholic schools); and school effects (various features of school operations that contribute to school life). In combination, analyzing data with respect to these three potential theoretical mechanisms suggested that it is the *coherence* of school life in Catholic schools that most clearly accounts for its relative success in this area. Nonetheless, controversy still exists about the circumstances when Catholic schools are superior, about how to control for family differences in the choice of schools, and about the policy implications of these findings.

researchers' analyses suggested that aspects of school life that enhance a sense of community within Catholic schools most effectively explained the differences in student outcomes between Catholic and public schools.

Exploring Mechanism When Theory Is Weak

When the theoretical basis for addressing questions related to mechanism is weak, contested, or poorly understood, other types of methods may be more appropriate. These queries often have strong descriptive components and derive their strength from in-depth study that can illuminate unforeseen relationships and generate new insights. We provide two examples in this section of such approaches: the first is the ethnographic study of college women (see Box 5-2) and the second is a "design study" that resulted in a theoretical model for how young children learn the mathematical concepts of ratio and proportion.

After generating a rich description of women's lives in their universities based on extensive analysis of ethnographic and survey data, the researchers turned to the question of *why* women who majored in nontraditional majors typically did not pursue those fields as careers (see Box 5-2). Was it because women were not well prepared before college? Were they discriminated against? Did they not want to compete with men? To address these questions, the researchers developed several theoretical models depicting commitment to schoolwork to describe how the women participated in college life. Extrapolating from the models, the researchers predicted what each woman would do after completing college, and in all cases, the models' predictions were confirmed.

A second example highlights another analytic approach for examining mechanism that begins with theoretical ideas that are tested through the design, implementation, and systematic study of educational tools (curriculum, teaching methods, computer applets) that embody the initial conjectured mechanism. The studies go by different names; perhaps the two most popular names are "design studies" (Brown, 1992) and "teaching experiments" (Lesh and Kelly, 2000; Schoenfeld, in press).

Box 5-5 illustrates a design study whose aim was to develop and elaborate the theoretical mechanism by which ratio reasoning develops in young children and to build and modify appropriate tasks and assessments that

BOX 5-5
Elementary School Students and Ratio and Proportion

In a project on student reasoning on ratio and proportion, Confrey and Lachance (2000) and colleagues examined a group of 20 students over a 3-year period in one classroom. Beginning with a conjecture about the relative independence of rational number structures (multiplication, division, ratio and proportion) from additive structures (addition and subtraction), the investigators sought the roots of ratio reasoning in a meaning of equivalence unfamiliar to the children. Consider how a 9-year-old might come to understand that 4:6 is equivalent to 6:9. Using a series of projects, tasks and challenges (such as designing a wheelchair access ramp or tourist guide to a foreign currency) researchers documented how students moved from believing that equivalence can be preserved through doubling (4:6 = 8:12) and halving (4:6 = 2:3), to the identification of a ratio unit (the smallest ratio to describe the equivalence in a set of proportions), to the ability to add and subtract ratio units (8:12 = 8+2: 12+3), to the ability to solve any ratio and proportion challenge in the familiar form $a:b :: c:x$.

This operational description of the mechanism behind ratio reasoning was used to develop instructional tasks—like calculating the slopes of the handicapped access ramps they had designed—and to observe students engaged in them. Classroom videotaping permitted researchers to review, both during the experiment and after its completion, the actual words, actions, and representations of students and teachers to build and elaborate the underlying conjectures about ratio reasoning.

At the same time, students' performance on mathematics assessments was compared with that of students in other classes and schools and to large-scale measures of performance on items designed to measure common misconceptions in ratio and proportion reasoning. The primary scientific product of the study was a theoretical model for ratio and proportion learning refined and enriched by years of in-depth study.

incorporate the models of learning developed through observation and interaction in the classroom. The work was linked to substantial existing literature in the field about the theoretical nature of ratio and proportion as mathematical ideas and teaching approaches to convey them (e.g., Behr, Lesh, Post, and Silver, 1983; Harel and Confrey, 1994; Mack, 1990, 1995). The initial model was tested and refined as careful distinctions and extensions were noted, explained, and considered as alternative explanations as the work progressed over a 3-year period, studying one classroom intensively. The design experiment methodology was selected because, unlike laboratory or other highly controlled approaches, it involved research within the complex interactions of teachers and students and allowed the everyday demands and opportunities of schooling to affect the investigation.

Like many such design studies, there were two main products of this work. First, through a theory-driven process of designing—and a data-driven process of refining—instructional strategies for teaching ratio and proportion, researchers produced an elaborated explanatory model of how young children come to understand these core mathematical concepts. Second, the instructional strategies developed in the course of the work itself hold promise because they were crafted based on a number of relevant research literatures. Through comparisons of achievement outcomes between children who received the new instruction and students in other classrooms and schools, the researchers provided preliminary evidence that the intervention designed to embody this theoretical mechanism is effective. The intervention would require further development, testing, and comparisons of the kind we describe in the previous section before it could be reasonably scaled up for widespread curriculum use.

Steffe and Thompson (2000) are careful to point out that design studies and teaching experiments must be conducted scientifically. In their words:

> We use experiment in "teaching experiment" in a scientific sense....
> What is important is that the teaching experiments are done to test
> hypotheses as well as to generate them. One does not embark on
> the intensive work of a teaching experiment without having major
> research hypotheses to test (p. 277).

This genre of method and approach is a relative newcomer to the field of education research and is not nearly as accepted as many of the other methods described in this chapter. We highlight it here as an illustrative example of the creative development of new methods to embed the complex instructional settings that typify U.S. education in the research process. We echo Steffe and Thompson's (2000) call to ensure a careful application of the scientific principles we describe in this report in the conduct of such research.[9]

CONCLUDING COMMENTS

This chapter, building on the scientific principles outlined in Chapter 3 and the features of education that influence their application in education presented in Chapter 4, illustrates that a wide range of methods can legitimately be employed in scientific education research and that some methods are better than others for particular purposes. As John Dewey put it:

> We know that some methods of inquiry are better than others in just the same way in which we know that some methods of surgery, arming, road-making, navigating, or what-not are better than others. It does not follow in any of these cases that the "better" methods are ideally perfect...We ascertain *how and why* certain means and agencies have provided warrantably assertible conclusions, while others have not and *cannot* do so (Dewey, 1938, p. 104, italics in original).

The chapter also makes clear that knowledge is generated through a sequence of interrelated descriptive and causal studies, through a constant process of refining theory and knowledge. These lines of inquiry typically require a range of methods and approaches to subject theories and conjectures to scrutiny from several perspectives.

We conclude this chapter with several observations and suggestions about the current state of education research that we believe warrant attention if scientific understanding is to advance beyond its current state. We do not provide a comprehensive agenda for the nation. Rather, we

---

[9]We are aware of several efforts, funded by both federal agencies and foundations, aimed at further development of this approach to ensure its standard and rigorous practice.

wish to offer constructive guidance by pointing to issues we have identified throughout our deliberations as key to future improvements.

First, there are a number of areas in education practice and policy in which basic theoretical understanding is weak. For example, very little is known about how young children learn ratio and proportion—mathematical concepts that play a key role in developing mathematical proficiency. The study we highlight in this chapter generated an initial theoretical model that must undergo sustained development and testing. In such areas, we believe priority should be given to descriptive and theory-building studies of the sort we highlight in this chapter. Scientific description is an essential part of any scientific endeavor, and education is no different. These studies are often extremely valuable in themselves, and they also provide the critical theoretical grounding needed to conduct causal studies. We believe that attention to the development and systematic testing of theories and conjectures across multiple studies and using multiple methods—a key scientific principle that threads throughout all of the questions and designs we have discussed—is currently undervalued in education relative to other scientific fields. The physical sciences have made progress by continuously developing and testing theories; something of that nature has not been done systematically in education. And while it is not clear that grand, unifying theories exist in the social world, conceptual understanding forms the foundation for scientific understanding and progresses—as we showed in Chapter 2—through the systematic assessment and refinement of theory.

Second, while large-scale education policies and programs are constantly undertaken, we reiterate our belief that they are typically launched without an adequate evidentiary base to inform their development, implementation, or refinement over time (Campbell, 1969; President's Committee of Advisors on Science and Technology, 1997). The "demand" for education research in general, and education program evaluation in particular, is very difficult to quantify, but we believe it tends to be low from educators, policy makers, and the public. There are encouraging signs that public attitudes toward the use of objective evidence to guide decisions is improving (e.g., statutory requirements to set aside a percentage of annual appropriations to conduct evaluations of federal programs, the Government Performance and Results Act, and common rhetoric about "evidence-based" and "research-based" policy and practice). However, we believe stronger scientific knowledge is needed about educational interventions to promote its use in decision making.

In order to generate a rich store of scientific evidence that could enhance effective decision making about education programs, it will be necessary to strengthen a few related strands of work. First, systematic study is needed about the ways that programs are implemented in diverse educational settings. We view implementation research—the genre of research that examines the ways that the structural elements of school settings interact with efforts to improve instruction—as a critical, underfunded, and underappreciated form of education research. We also believe that understanding how to "scale up" (Elmore, 1996) educational interventions that have promise in a small number of cases will depend critically on a deep understanding of how policies and practices are adopted and sustained (Rogers, 1995) in the complex U.S. education system.[10]

In all of this work, more knowledge is needed about causal relationships. In estimating the effects of programs, we urge the expanded use of random assignment. Randomized experiments are not perfect. Indeed, the merits of their use in education have been seriously questioned (Cronbach et al., 1980; Cronbach, 1982; Guba and Lincoln, 1981). For instance, they typically cannot test complex causal hypotheses, they may lack generalizability to other settings, and they can be expensive. However, we believe that these and other issues do not generate a compelling rationale against their use in education research and that issues related to ethical concerns, political obstacles, and other potential barriers often can be resolved. We believe that the credible objections to their use that have been raised have clarified the purposes, strengths, limitations, and uses of randomized experiments as well as other research methods in education. Establishing cause is often exceedingly important—for example, in the large-scale deployment of interventions—and the ambiguity of correlational studies or quasi-experiments can be undesirable for practical purposes.

In keeping with our arguments throughout this report, we also urge that randomized field trials be supplemented with other methods, including in-depth qualitative approaches that can illuminate important nuances,

---

[10]The federal Interagency Education Research Initiative was developed to tackle this thorny issue.

identify potential counterhypotheses, and provide additional sources of evidence for supporting causal claims in complex educational settings.

In sum, theory building and rigorous studies of implementations and interventions are two broad-based areas that we believe deserve attention. Within the framework of a comprehensive research agenda, targeting these aspects of research will build on the successes of the enterprise we highlight throughout this report.

6

Design Principles for Fostering Science in a Federal Education Research Agency

The federal government has an important and legitimate role in sup-porting research as a public good, including research in education (e.g., National Research Council, 1999d; President's Committee of Advisors on Science and Technology, 1997; Geweke and Straf, 1999). The federal government's role in education research dates back to the middle of the nineteenth century, when the U.S. Department of Education was established[1] to collect statistics and provide exemplary models for the nation's schools. Then as now, the nation recognized the value of centrally gener-ated education research that should be made available to all states, districts, and schools. In the absence of a federal leadership role, knowledge gained by one state or district that might be relevant to others would not likely be widely distributed, as individual states tend to undervalue the benefits that would accrue to others. Moreover, many scientific studies contrast alternative education approaches or models, and important comparisons are frequently made across states, districts, and schools. The federal govern-ment is also the natural place to collect and make data widely available on education performance, costs, processes, inputs, and their interrelationships.

---

[1] The U.S. Department of Education was first formed in 1867; its name was changed to the Bureau of Education shortly thereafter and later to the Office of Education. The modern U.S. Department of Education was established in 1979.

Assuming a legitimate federal role in education research, this chapter addresses the question: How should a federal education research agency be designed to foster scientific research in education, given the complexities of the practice of education, the stringencies of the scientific principles, and the wide range of legitimate research designs?

While our focus is on design principles for a single agency, we point out that education research of national interest has historically been supported by several offices in the U.S. Department of Education, by other agencies of the federal government, and by private organizations (e.g., foundations). A federal agency is only one part of this larger enterprise, but it occupies a central place within it. Indeed, while the committee makes a number of suggestions for one agency to lead the scientific enterprise, we recognize that some of the tasks might best be conducted in partnership with other agencies or nongovernmental organizations, and we encourage the exploration of such options. Within this broader context of scientific research in education, this chapter takes up the specific issue of how a federal research agency might be designed to best fulfill its role in the scientific enterprise.

Our approach in this chapter is forward looking. Throughout, we speak of a generic agency because the committee wanted to free its deliberations from exclusive consideration of the current incumbent, the U.S. Department of Education's Office of Educational Research and Improvement (OERI). Although this report is in part intended to help policy makers think about the pending reauthorization of OERI, *the committee was not charged with, nor did it conduct, an evaluation of OERI.* Rather, we relied on data we have collected from a sampling of federal social science research agencies and programs—including OERI—about how they support their science missions.[2] In short, while we reiterate that we did not evaluate OERI, we clearly could not avoid learning about it or discussing it, especially in a comparative way, to address our charge effectively. Thus,

---

[2]Specifically, we collected data from OERI, the Social, Behavioral, and Economic Sciences and Education and Human Resources Directorates at the National Science Foundation, the Child Development and Behavior Branch at the National Institute on Child Health and Human Development, and the Social and Behavioral Research Program at the National Institute on Aging.

throughout this chapter we refer to OERI and other agencies, most often comparing various aspects of funding and operations among them.

We also relied on information the committee gathered at a workshop it sponsored in March 2001 that featured panels of senior officials from these and other agencies as well as knowledgeable experts about the federal role. The participants discussed the federal role in education research and related social sciences across several agencies with an eye toward the future of a federal education research agency (again, OERI was one of several agencies represented and discussed). This event is summarized in a workshop report (see National Research Council, 2001d).

Based on the information gathered at the workshop and through subsequent data collection, our guiding principles of science, the features of education that influence the conduct of research, and the nature of scientific progression, we develop six design principles around the notion of creating a *scientific culture*. We argue throughout this report that science itself is supported through the norms and mores of the scientific community, and we believe that cultivating these values within a research agency is the key to its success. We also note that decades of organizational fixes at the current agency have arguably not done much to improve its culture and, consequently, its reputation.

Our focus on a scientific culture within an agency stems from the recognition that an agency in many ways reflects the field it supports, and vice versa. An agency's success requires a strong group of scholars, and the broader community depends in part on a vibrant federal presence. Thus, our design principles emphasize the role of researchers to lead and staff the agency, to serve on advisory boards, to help synthesize the current state of knowledge, and to act as peer reviewers of proposals and programs of research. The principles also recognize the role of the agency in building the professional capacity of the field.

Other themes in this report are embedded in the design principles as well. For example, we take up the issue of research ethics—an influential aspect of the education research enterprise (see Chapter 4)—from the perspective of the federal regulations that govern them. We also argue for flexible decision-making authority in the agency to accommodate the dynamic nature of scientific progress and opportunity (see Chapters 2 and 3). And we suggest the agency attempt to enhance part of its research portfolio by finding ways to bring it closer to the complexities of educational practice (see Chapter 4).

It is important to recognize the difference between this focus on developing a scientific culture and the focus on research methods in H.R. 4875[3]—the bill that at least in part led to this report—and several related debates about the future of OERI. The language in the bill contains many of the key concepts we treat in this report, including systematic data collection, experimentation, rigorous reasoning, replication, and peer review. However, attempting to boost the scientific basis of federally funded education research by mandating a list of "valid" scientific methods is a problematic strategy. The inclusion of a list of methods—regardless of how they are applied in particular situations—erroneously assumes that science is mechanistic and thus can be prescribed. We have shown that science adheres to a set of common principles but its application depends greatly on the particulars of a given situation and the objects of inquiry. The definitions also make clear distinctions between quantitative and qualitative methods, implying that these two types of research approaches are fundamentally different; we argue the opposite. Furthermore, the use of definitions of methods as a tool for improvement fails to recognize the crucial role of theory and, as we emphasize, a strong, self-regulated, skeptical community of researchers that pushes the boundaries of knowledge. It is in this spirit that we focus on scientific culture in approaching the design of a federal education research agency.

The committee recognizes an inherent dilemma in designing an agency to support scientific research in education. Scientific education research is often grounded in the practical problems of teaching, learning, and schooling and their varied contexts. Therefore, it is important to engage practitioners in the functions of the agency and to link research to the design and management of federal education programs. However, as we describe below, history has shown that a close bureaucratic relationship between research and educational programming in a federal agency can overwhelm the research function. Thus, we attempt to clarify the proper roles of researchers, practitioners, and politicians to ensure the needs of these com-

---

[3]To view the text of the bill, go to http://thomas.loc.gov/ and search for H.R. 4875 in the 106th Congress.

munities are met and their strengths maximized. We believe strongly that the responsibility for the success of the agency and the broader research effort it supports lies not solely with federal policy makers, but is shared among all those who have a stake in education and education research.

Another dilemma has to do with the composition of the education research community itself. As we argue earlier in this report, we believe that the vast diversity that characterizes the field of education research is both a great strength and a troubling weakness. The variation in epistemological paradigms, methodological tools, and professional training lends the enterprise intellectual vitality. This same variation, however, is a source of cultural divisions among subfields that fosters isolation and impedes scientific consensus building and progress. In short, the "community" of scientists in education is really an eclectic mix of scholars with different norms and different standards of evidence. While we talk about the scientific community and its role in a federal agency as if it were a unified, easily identifiable group, the reality is more complex. The talent pool in education research is shaped by a number of structural, historical, and cultural variables, and parsing them out requires careful analysis. Thus, in the discussion that follows, we attempt to highlight issues that may be relevant in the implementation of the design principles vis-à-vis the field.

Our vision is that the fundamental mission of a federal education research agency would be to promote and protect the integrity of scientific research in education with the goal of generating knowledge that can inform policy and practice decisions.[4] To achieve this mission, the agency needs to develop and nurture a scientific culture, and to do so, it must have an infrastructure, supported by sufficient resources, that enables a cadre of experienced staff to make decisions flexibly and to interact continuously

---

[4]Although our focus is on scientific research, we believe that the federal government should also fund related activities, such as development and demonstration work, a statistics function, a national library, other forms of educational scholarship (e.g., history and philosophy), and a research dissemination and implementation structure. Scientific research is related to, and often depends on, these functions. Indeed, we believe that it is the integration of scientific knowledge with insights from the humanities and other scholarly pursuits that will ultimately yield the most powerful understanding of education. However, we do not address them explicitly in this report because they are outside the scope of the committee's charge to focus on scientific research in education.

with the field it supports. We develop six design principles from these core ideas:

- Staff the agency with people skilled in science, leadership, and management.
- Create structures to guide agenda, inform funding decisions, and monitor work.
- Insulate the agency from inappropriate political interference.
- Develop a focused and balanced portfolio of research that addresses short-, medium-, and long-term issues of importance to policy and practice.
- Adequately fund the agency.
- Invest in research infrastructure.

The rest of this chapter elaborates these principles and provides suggestions for specific mechanisms that could be implemented to support them. We stress that these suggestions do not reflect a view that there is one "model" that dictates the specific design features of any federal research agency. Indeed, the U.S. federal research enterprise is characterized by a range of structures and processes that is effective in respected agencies across the federal government (National Research Council, 2001d; Mathtech, 1996).

DESIGN PRINCIPLE 1
Staff the Agency with People Skilled in Science, Leadership, and Management

We begin with leadership and staffing deliberately: a scientific culture begins (and ends) with competent people. Attracting and retaining an adequate number of qualified leaders and staff is so critical to a healthy federal education research agency that we believe without it, little else matters. There is no substitute for leadership and human capacity.

The leaders of the agency are of paramount importance. All federal agency leaders need leadership and management skills and, for this agency, the leaders—political appointees and career officials alike—must be respected educational researchers with strong scientific credentials. The culture of an organization emanates from its leaders; without research experience at the top levels, the norms and mores of science will likely not take hold.

Similarly, the agency's research staff should have extensive education research experience. They must have knowledge of relevant content as well as be able to recognize scientifically rigorous design, theory, data collection strategies, and analysis techniques. The agency should employ a mix of research staff, where promising junior scholars work alongside senior research staff to infuse new ideas into the agency's work and to develop future senior staff of the agency. Providing ongoing professional development opportunities for research staff is also critical to allow continuing and sustained interaction with the broader research community.

How can a federal education research agency attract and retain such human resources to develop and maintain a scientific culture that fosters and protects the integrity of scientifically rigorous research in education? This is a difficult question.

In keeping with the range of hiring strategies of several existing federal research agencies,[5] a federal education research agency should have the authority to pursue multiple approaches to develop its leadership and staff. Developing a core of permanent staff offers the benefit of increasing institutional knowledge and long-term relationships within the government and the research field. Short-term assignments can serve the dual purpose of updating the agency with new ideas from the field and acquainting university faculty and other researchers with the operations, needs, and

---

[5]While all federal personnel actions are governed by Title V of the United States Code, many research agencies have exemptions from certain provisions regarding hiring practices to be able to retain the services of temporary scientific or technical employees. Within these parameters, agencies staff their organizations in very different ways. In the Social, Behavioral, and Economic Sciences Directorate at the U.S. National Science Foundation (NSF), for example, 40 percent of the current research staff is comprised of several types of temporary "rotators" who work in the directorate for a short time. These temporary appointments have historically been used to bring the expertise and perspective of active researchers into the operations of the agency. The Child Development and Behavior Branch of the National Institute for Child Health and Human Development (NICHD) at the National Institutes of Health (NIH), in contrast, has had only three short-term staff appointments since 1995; instead, it depends on permanent staff to convene workshops with those in the field for the purpose of ensuring it is in touch with the perspective of active researchers.

accomplishments of the agency. For similar reasons, the appointment of postdoctoral fellows can be beneficial. These appointments also help build the capacity of future leaders in the research field.

Another way for a federal education research agency to cultivate scientific norms in its staff is to engage in collaborative research efforts with other agencies to encourage interaction with staff who have traditions of supporting related scientific work. Such collaborations can enrich the breadth and depth of staff knowledge, and they also offer the benefit of developing cutting-edge, interdisciplinary research programs across federal agencies (National Research Council, 1999d). There are several current interagency efforts in education research from which lessons could be learned: examples include the Interagency Education Research Initiative, a partnership of OERI, NICHD, and NSF aimed at understanding how to scale up promising education practices, and a joint OERI-NICHD initiative focused on understanding how best to help bilingual students learn to read in English.

Although these policy tools can help attract and retain top staff, staffing will depend heavily on related issues, such as funding, reputation, and leadership. For example, to the extent that education research is underfunded relative to other opportunities available to researchers (see Design Principle 5 below), top talent will likely go elsewhere, both in the field and in the agency. The early 1980s provides a lesson. With significant federal budget cuts in education and social science research, researchers migrated, especially to the health and national defense fields, many never to return. These funding deficiencies have affected OERI's ability to attract and retain a cadre of capable staff despite having hiring authority similar to NSF and NIH. Staff levels were reduced drastically in the 1980s as a result of deep federal budget cuts, but even as its funding began to climb in the 1990s, the agency again lost 25 percent of its staff, including some of the most capable and experienced individuals (Vinovskis, 2000).

The reputation of an agency and its leadership will also affect staffing. Developing a good reputation, of course, is not a simple matter of policy fixes. Adequate funding will help, but if the agency suffers from a poor reputation, its leaders will have to be creative about staffing possibilities and may need to convince a critical mass of researchers to serve at the same time. In this vein, the development of a scientific culture is critical; initial appointments have to be highly talented researchers who, in addition to being offered very attractive positions, should be encouraged to view such federal service as an important way to strengthen their profession.

DESIGN PRINCIPLE 2
Create Structures to Guide Agenda, Inform Funding Decisions, and Monitor Work

To accomplish its core tasks, a federal education research agency must be supported by a coherent system of governance. While we do not offer a comprehensive plan, we do believe that two essential elements of such a structure have the highest probability of cultivating scientific norms both inside and outside the agency: a high-level governing board and standing peer review panels of top-flight scientists.

Governing Board

Governing boards are common management and oversight tools for federal research agencies. We believe that particular attention to aspects of the board's composition and responsibilities can further the development of a scientific culture within the agency as well as foster interactions with other stakeholders. We suggest that the agency operate under the general direction of a high-level governing board, drawn from leaders in education policy and practice, education research, business, and both political parties. The diversity of the governing board will allow the many different cultures associated with each representative group to learn from one another as they work toward common goals. Many research agencies currently have some kind of a governing or advisory board (e.g., the National Science Board of the NSF and OERI's National Educational Research Policy and Priorities Board [NERPPB]). Such a board should provide advice to senior leadership, recommend research directions, help to safeguard the independence of the agency, provide critical links to practice and policy communities, and reinforce scientific norms inside the agency.

A key task of this board would be to develop the research agenda. No matter how strong its science, if the agency does not carefully develop and maintain its agenda in close collaboration with researchers, policy makers, and practitioners and in alignment with available resources, it will fail to meet its mission. The challenges facing American education—low achievement levels, cost, growing numbers of second-language learners—are very real and demand serious investment. For education research to play a role, it is imperative that a federal education research agency have clear, long-term priorities for generating knowledge and promoting its transfer and utilization to engage the field in a collaborative effort toward understanding core issues in education.

The agency might also include an agenda-setting committee, chaired by a distinguished practitioner, which would work with the board on the research agenda. Representatives from the scientific community should serve to help identify areas that warrant further research on the basis of the state of scientific development; this task may involve identifying areas of research that are ripe for immediate testing, or that require more basic descriptive research to generate scientific hypotheses or assertions. Representatives from the practice communities should serve to articulate the high-priority issues for educational improvement from a practical perspective. And representatives from the policy communities should serve to articulate short and enduring policy issues, as well as the feasibility of moving in new directions as recommended by researchers and practitioners.

Another role for a governing board would be to report to Congress and the nation on the agency's progress toward clearly stated and commonly shared goals. In the spirit of the 1993 Government Performance and Results Act (GPRA), the agency should be accountable for research results: knowledge generation and dissemination. Since research results are difficult to quantify, federal research agencies have struggled to comply with this law. A recent report (National Research Council, 1999b) provides some guidance on how to assess the outcomes of research for GPRA reporting. Plans and measures should be developed according to the character of the research program and acknowledge (as we do in this report) that the progression of science is jagged and often unexpected.

Standing Peer Review Panels

Peer review is the single most typically used mechanism for nurturing a scientific culture within and outside federal research agencies, and one that should play a feature role in a federal education research agency. In the ideal, peer review is both a *process* by which scientific work is assessed and funded and a *product* in that it provides a venue for the scientific culture of self-regulation (Chubin and Hackett, 1990) we describe throughout this report. The process works on several levels. First, by involving a group of active researchers, the current state of the art is introduced and used in judging proposed research. Second, especially when used as a feedback mechanism for the field (National Research Council, 2001d), the review process itself encourages the development of an active community of scientists working together on education problems: the process of reviewing proposals and communicating feedback fosters the development of common standards of quality and other scientific norms in the field over time. Third, the peer-review process acts as a buffer against outside political pressures to choose certain proposals or fund certain researchers regardless of scientific merit.

A wide variety of peer review structures—ad hoc review committees, standing panels, mixture of outside and panel evaluations, and the like— can work. Indeed, the current federal system is characterized by this diversity of approaches (U.S. Government Accounting Office, 1999). For example, NIH uses both standing "study sections" and ad hoc review groups, while NSF and OERI only use ad hoc panels of reviewers for each competition. In contrast, the Office of Naval Research does not use panels of peer reviewers to fund proposals but rather regards its staff as peers able to make such decisions internally (National Research Council, 2001d).

We believe that a federal education research agency ought to use standing review panels akin to the NIH study sections as its primary peer review vehicle. We envision these standing panels as providing continuity in overseeing research programs (see Design Principle 4). This suggestion reinforces the recommendations of several other groups (that are studying OERI in particular), including the RAND panels (see http://www.rand.org/multi/achievementforall/) and the NERPPB in its policy statements (National Educational Research Policy and Priorities Board, 2000). When researchers join peer review panels that have a life over a period of years, panel members strengthen their knowledge and the panel as a whole develops an integrated, communal expertise. Members then communicate this knowledge to their colleagues through their review of proposals and interaction with colleagues, and they also demand that, in the proposals they review, the research community is up to date on the most recent synthesis of knowledge.

We caution that peer review is not a perfect quality assurance mechanism, and it can go wrong. History has shown that it can be a conservative instrument for selecting research proposals for funding, and can stifle innovation as a result (Cicchetti, 1991). To mitigate these problems, the agency's standing panels should have rotating membership terms to ensure that fresh perspectives are regularly replenished.

Whatever the structure and management of peer review panels, their successful implementation will require diligence and care with respect to their composition. For peer review to work well, the choice of peers is vital. By peers, we mean scientists conducting research in an education area that substantially overlaps with that of the proposals under review and, importantly, who can think beyond their own line of work. Since the topical areas under any particular competition can be quite vast, sometimes it is not possible to achieve total representation of topical areas (August and Muraskin, 1999). Therefore, it is critical to ensure the peers can think broadly. The goal is to assemble reviewers who have both the substantive and methodological knowledge to make science-based judgment about the merits of competing proposals and the state of current understanding. As a result, we believe that policy makers and practitioners should not have responsibility for judging the scientific merit of research proposals; they should have opportunities for ongoing collaborations in the agency, but not as part of peer review panels (see "Governing Board," above). This makes clear that agency staff must be adept at selecting and attracting appropriate individuals and achieving balance in groups of peer reviewers.

Furthermore, engaging the scientific community in the course of research planning and progress through peer review depends critically on an ample talent pool of peers. In the short term, one important consideration is the need to engage a range of perspectives relevant to the work. Agency leaders have to ensure that the collective membership of these panels does not bring a narrow view to the work. At the same time, the choice of peers must maximize the intellectual caliber and scientific expertise of the group. An overemphasis on ensuring broad content area, epistemological, and methodological representation can backfire if such considerations outweigh the overarching need to engage top scientific talent in the effort. In sum, assembling the right group is a finely nuanced task. Ultimately, the long-term viability of standing panels or other mechanisms for peer review in scientific education research will depend on sustained attention to building the capacity of the field itself (see Design Principle 6 below).

We have focused thus far on the issues of peers and peer review from the perspective of a federal agency. However, the responsibility to assemble high-quality panels in the short term and to enhance the profession in the long term does not rest solely with the federal government. Indeed, we believe the community of researchers plays the most critical role in making peer review work. It is the professional responsibility of scientists to participate in efforts that promote scientific collaboration, consultation, and critique. A federal agency is a natural place to engage in that work. The future of the field—and the federal agency that supports it—will depend in no small part on finding new ways to harness the scholarly potential of its diverse perspectives.

DESIGN PRINCIPLE 3
Insulate the Agency from Inappropriate Political Interference

A federal education research agency must be designed to prevent inappropriate political criteria from entering into the agency's agenda for research, its choice of research studies, its selection of grantees, and its scientific norms. Ensuring that political interference is minimal will foster a scientific culture, protect the scientific process, and prevent research from being sacrificed to the policy passions and practice fads of the day. While we are agnostic about where in the federal government an education research agency should reside, it must have a large degree of independence from partisan politics from both the executive and legislative branches of government.

We want to be clear that buffering the agency from politics in the U.S. system cannot, and should not, be total. However desirable the autonomy of the agency might be from a scientific perspective, its research agenda must be responsive to the needs of decision makers in education. Although research should not be driven only by the needs of the moment—say, school-based management one year, charter schools the next, standards and accountability the year after—proper attention must be paid to political concerns.

Nonetheless, there are specific kinds of political interference from which a federal education research agency must be insulated. They include micromanagement of decision making, the distortion of the research agenda to be solely short-run, and the use of the agency as a tool to promote a particular policy or position—problems that occur with some frequency across research agencies (Vinovskis, 2000; National Research Council, 1992). To protect the agency from these influences, we suggest that it have independent authority for hiring, disbursal of funds, and publishing. We also urge that agency staff be trusted to make decisions based on their best judgments—informed by frequent interaction with the field—about scientific opportunity. In addition, we believe that the head of the agency should serve a fixed term that spans political administrations. Finally, a consistent fiscal resource commitment would help protect the agency from partisan budget decisions (see Design Principle 5).

Budgetary discretion is a particularly important area in light of the federal government's funding patterns for previous education research agencies (the National Institute of Education and OERI) over the last few decades. Two trends are noteworthy. First, in the Behavioral and Social Research Program at the National Institute on Aging (NIA), the Child Development and Behavior Branch at the NICHD, and the Social, Behavioral, and Economic Sciences and Education and Human Resources Directorates at NSF, staff had the freedom to develop programs and solicit proposals for a significant proportion of their fiscal 2000 research budgets. By contrast, how OERI's roughly $130 million research budget will be spent is largely determined by requirements in its current authorizing statute. This legislation requires that at least 25 percent of the annual appropriation for research fund field-initiated studies and at least 15 percent fund research centers.[6] Our review of a sample of research agency authorizing statutes showed that no other research agency is subject to such legal requirements

---

[6]Of the approximately $130 million in research funds in fiscal 2000, roughly $85 million is managed through five internal institutes, and the remainder is embedded in the regional laboratory structure and other improvement activities. The congressionally mandated percentages we cite here apply to the institute funds.

about its use of funds. Furthermore, at our public workshop in March 2001 (National Research Council, 2001d), we heard repeatedly—from three former assistant secretaries, a branch chief at another agency who works with OERI on an interagency research program, and several OERI staff—that a lack of flexibility was a significant problem in OERI. A federal education research agency must have the discretion to invest the bulk of its appropriations in its scientific research agenda to effectively manage evolving research programs. We believe that Congress should have the ability to review the outcomes of the research (see Design Principle 2) and to make appropriations decisions based on performance over time. It should not, however, require that funds be allocated through specific mechanisms or earmark funds for unreviewed projects.

Second, the current federal education research agency, OERI, includes several large nonresearch, service-oriented programs such that its research mission is compromised (National Research Council, 1992). The original intent of including the "I" in OERI (that is, the school improvement function) was to forge a close relationship between cutting-edge research and program funds aimed at improving schools. While in the abstract this idea made good sense, a school improvement agenda can overwhelm the agency's fiscal and intellectual capacity to focus on its core research mission. While total funding (in 2000 dollars) for OERI has increased nearly tenfold between 1980 and 2000, the percentage of its budget that funds its core research mission fell sharply in the early 1980s and has since remained at roughly 15 percent. The lion's share of its monies has funded service-oriented programs to states, school districts, and schools to implement "research-based" reform. This trend is also evident at NSF's Education and Human Resources (EHR) Directorate, which also houses a mix of education reform programs and research. Since 1980, EHR's budget has risen substantially (from $163 million in fiscal 1980 to $691 million in fiscal 2000 [in 2000 dollars]), but the proportion of its total appropriation that funds research has been meager, ranging from 2.2 to 7.7 percent.[7]

---

[7]Most EHR program grants—as distinct from research grants—include small amounts for research. Since the figures we present here reflect a strict categorization of projects based on their primary purpose (i.e., research or services), the estimated percentage of the total agency budget dedicated to research is slightly understated.

The trends at these two hybrid organizations strongly suggest that the research function of a federal education research agency should be organizationally separate from an educational improvement mission, leaving the latter to a parallel entity with its own budget. A measure of bureaucratic distance between these two functions is also desirable because it would be difficult to develop a common culture in an education research agency given the appropriate differences between research and program administration.

These potential benefits notwithstanding, it is essential that the research agency forge close links with an improvement entity to foster the integration of research-based insights into the design and implementation of service-oriented education programs at all levels. We leave open the question of what form such an educational improvement organization should take (e.g., regional institutes), but do make some suggestions about the infrastructure needed to better connect research and practice (see Design Principle 6).

DESIGN PRINCIPLE 4
Develop a Focused and Balanced Portfolio of Research That Addresses Short-, Medium-, and Long-Term Issues of Importance to Policy and Practice

Scientific research must focus on the challenges confronting education—increasing achievement for all learners, teaching children science in classrooms where 5 to 15 different languages are spoken, creating opportunities where access to rigorous education has been blocked, and other pressing, difficult problems facing educators. While these needs and pressures will be strong, the agency is sure to fail if it attempts to produce "quick solutions to poorly understood problems" (National Research Council, 1992, p. viii).

A federal education research agency must have the freedom to go beyond the short-term view and make long-term investments in promising lines of research that have reasonable probability of helping to solve important practical problems and generating new and refined theoretical frameworks. It must have the freedom to address topics that may not accord with political opinion or administration policy. More generally, the research agenda must be aligned to reflect an understanding of its developmental phase. This assertion does not suggest that education researchers lower their standards for rigor, but rather that resources and investigations need to be targeted according to a frank assessment of the formative developmental character of the field. Thus, the agency should support a balanced research portfolio with the goal of building theoretical frameworks to undergird the research enterprise and the long-term capacity of research programs to anticipate, as well as address, the pressing needs of policy and practice. Striking the right balance is the key to a successful research portfolio.

In Chapter 2 we show that science-based knowledge accumulates when a field is organized around, and works toward understanding of, a particular question, theory, or problem. With some notable exceptions, the current education research enterprise is highly fragmented (Lagemann, 2000; Vinovskis, 2000; National Research Council, 1992). A new agency must lead the field by focusing scientific research on clearly defined, long-term, strategically focused programs of research with the goal of producing cumulative findings about pressing problems in education (see http:// www.rand.org/multi/achievementforall/; National Research Council, 1999d). Moreover, the research portfolio should be use-inspired (Stokes, 1997), including a mix of fundamental science and applied questions; projects with short-, mid-, and long-term horizons; and a variety of research types and methods.

To achieve this balance, we suggest that the agency develop constellations of related research projects, or programs. For example, schools under externally mandated accountability requirements are searching for curricula and teaching methods to boost all students' science achievement on a variety of outcomes (e.g., tests, course-taking, grades, and other formative measures). A program of research focused on this challenge might support short-term syntheses of what is known, mid-term evaluations of promising programs, and long-term studies of the acquisition and development of science competence.

The development of research programs holds promise for several reasons. First, in areas where there has been sustained support for research (like the example of early reading skills we highlight in Chapter 2), there is a clear progression of education research findings. For example, the Office of Naval Research began funding studies on advanced educational technology in 1969, and it is only in the last few years—30 years later—that this investment has yielded applicable results (National Research Council, 2001d). Second, establishing programs with a long-term view focuses the agenda and develops an infrastructure for research to progressively move toward scientific consensus.

While long-term research should be an important part of an agency's programs, that portfolio should also include shorter range challenges. One way of addressing immediate challenges is by summarizing existing research related to a particular topic or problem. Indeed, research syntheses, consensus panels, literature reviews, and other kinds of summary statements about a body of work are important because conflicting evidence across individual studies in education is a major source of frustration among education policy makers and practitioners (see e.g., Sroufe, 1997). Studies that reach different conclusions about the same topic are commonplace, not only in education research, but also in many sciences (e.g., experimental ecology) and many fields (e.g., public health) (National Research Council, 2001d). But this fact does little to placate policy makers and practitioners who often must make decisions or take action on the basis of available information.

Perhaps more importantly, a federal education research agency should systematically conduct research syntheses as part of their program work in order to build scientific consensus by supporting thorough, balanced reviews of research selected from studies that meet scientific criteria. As we describe in Chapter 2, these syntheses provide a mechanism for the accumulation of research-based knowledge. Statistical syntheses (e.g., Glass and Smith, 1978; Hedges and Olkin, 1983; Hedges, Laine, and Greenwald, 1994) provide a means of aggregating across studies. Such syntheses depend on statistical sampling and design quality standards and attend to scientific principles of reproducibility, transparency in standards of evidence, estimation of the role of chance and variation, and the wide availability of findings to invite professional critique (peer review).

At times, however, even statistical syntheses produce conflicting evidence (as was the case with class-size reduction effects; see Chapter 3). Thus, the agency should also support a complementary synthesis method— consensus panels that synthesize bodies of work. Such panels bring together scholars with diverse perspectives and experiences on an issue. They are charged with amassing the best knowledge and wisdom in an area and using clear standards of evidence for selecting and interpreting studies. Such panels must also adhere to scientific principles of transparency of method, assessing uncertainty, and subjecting findings to the skeptical eye of the broader scientific community. They can be a natural parallel approach with statistical syntheses. Such groups of experts working together can propel science forward by forcing groups of scholars with different perspectives and expertise to confront one another in a healthy, scholarly debate toward the advancement of theoretical, methodological, and empirical understanding.

The extent to which such reviews are conducted in federal research agencies varies considerably. The Child Development and Behavior Branch at NICHD and the Behavioral and Social Research Program at NIA both produce research reviews annually; OERI and the Social, Behavioral, and Economic Sciences and Education and Human Resources Directorates at NSF have no formal mechanism for review and synthesis. We believe that the fact that federal agencies (and foundations) that support education research typically do not view synthesis as their primary responsibility must change if knowledge in education is to grow substantially. Indeed, in the absence of regular efforts to synthesize knowledge, several new entities whose sole aim is to synthesize what is known about a particular topic, problem, or intervention have been created in recent years or are in their planning stages (e.g., Campbell Collaboration [see Box 2-1], Education Quality Institute, and a potential new center of the Pew Charitable Trusts).

Finally, these programs ought to include investments in the scientific study of effective modes of dissemination and implementation of the research. We view the critical issue of research utilization as not only a role for a federal education research agency, but also as an area much in need of sustained scientific study itself.

In addition to developing coherent programs, infusing new, cutting-edge, innovative lines of inquiry into a research portfolio also should be an important function of a federal research agency. To this end, the agency should support a healthy program of field-initiated studies outside of the scope of its pre-defined programs.

DESIGN PRINCIPLE 5
Adequately Fund the Agency

The call for higher levels of funding for education research is hardly new (National Research Council, 2001d, 1999d; President's Committee of Advisers on Science and Technology, 1997; Shavelson and Berliner, 1988; Vinovskis, 2000; Fuhrman, 2001; Schmidt, 2001; Forgione, 2001). We include it among our design principles for this reason: although we did not conduct an analysis of the quality of federally funded education research, we agree with those who came before us that funding has not historically been aligned with the intended scope of the education research enterprise. Given our assumption that the agenda of a federal education research agency will be roughly comparable to what it has been in the past, coupled with the obvious recommendation that resources be aligned with the scope and expectations of the enterprise, it follows that we recommend increased appropriations to ensure that the agency can adequately meet its mandate.

For background on these recommendations, we briefly review available data and literature related to the federal investment in education research. Unfortunately, no reliable estimates exist of the total investment in education research (Morrill, 1998; National Research Council, 1992). It is difficult even to ascertain how much is invested at the federal level due to problems categorizing research projects across the many agencies and sub-agencies that fund education research. In 1997 the President's Committee of Advisors on Science and Technology published a report that attempted to sum the federal investment across agencies based on 1995 dollars. It found that less than one-tenth of 1 percent (<0.001) of the total amount the U.S. spent on K-12 education was invested in research. By contrast, it reported that 23 percent of the amount spent on prescription and nonprescription medication was invested in drug development and testing. Similarly, the National Research Council (1999d) concluded that compared to other knowledge-dependent fields, there has been remarkably little invested in the systematic, scientific study of education.

Further evidence of the inadequacy of funding comes from a comparative assessment of research funding in federal agencies. The data we collected from OERI and four similar agencies and organizations helped us gauge (in a rough sense) the ratios of funding level to the scope of the agenda. Comparing the breadth of research agendas alongside annual funding in this way, we find a stark contrast between OERI and other federal social science research outfits across the federal government. The substantial and long-term investment made by NICHD in early reading research, for example, has reaped a significant return for the agency and the nation. NICHD has invested a total of $100 million over 30 years specifically to better understand phonological awareness and related early reading competencies. It was only through this substantial, sustained investment that, in conjunction with significant funding and intellectual contributions by other federal agencies (e.g., the Office of Special Education Programs in the U.S. Department of Education) and other countries, the research in this relatively focused area has been able to grow.

By contrast, the scope of OERI's research mandate is sweeping and its funding level modest. Its 1994 reauthorization established five institutes within the agency that roughly sketched its agenda. These five institutes include such broad categories as student achievement, students at risk of educational failure, education policy, early childhood, and postsecondary and life-long learning, and fund research through a range of mechanisms (e.g., centers, field-initiated studies). Each of these institutes spans academic subject areas (e.g., reading, mathematics, science, history) and in many cases educational levels (e.g., student achievement, policy, and at risk all span pre-K through adult learning). This categorization is a reasonable way to parse the field, and we would expect any federal education research agency to cover a similar breadth of content. However, it is unreasonable to expect that robust, research-based knowledge could grow out of them given the fact that roughly $130 million per year (fiscal 2000 level) must cover this broad scope.

Over the course of its history, the primary research agency has had roughly the same agenda but large differences in funding levels. A 1992 National Research Council report charted the precipitous drop in funding for the National Institute of Education (NIE, predecessor agency to OERI) and OERI between 1973 and 1991. In 1973, NIE's total budget was $136 million ($527.5 million in 2000 constant dollars). By 1991, only $78.4 million ($99.1 million in 2000 constant dollars) of OERI's budget was allocated to research. This substantial drop in funding occurred with no commensurate change in the scope of its agenda. The report argued that OERI's limited resources had been spread "so thinly that mediocrity was almost assured. Only a few lines of research have been sustained for the time they needed to bring them to fruition" (National Research Council, 1992, p. 3). To put this mismatch in dollars into perspective, the Tennessee STAR study (see Box 3-3), a single investigation in a single state that spanned 4 years, cost $10 million over its lifetime.

Although total funding at OERI (adjusted for inflation) has risen substantially, nearly all of the increase has funded service-oriented programs with only tenuous connections to research. Since 1990, there has been a slight rebound in total education research funding, with the fiscal 2000 level at approximately $130 million (including nonresearch activities, OERI's fiscal budget exceeds $800 million). We view this trend as positive, but believe that given the current breadth of the education research agenda, future increases will be necessary.

In sum, we believe that if a federal education research agency is to have an agenda at least as ambitious in scope as its predecessors', its funding must be higher than these agencies have had in the past. At the risk of overstating the obvious, we wish to make clear that this is *not* a call to simply "throw more money at research." Money alone will not ensure the creation and accumulation of high-quality science-based knowledge in education— or any other field. Increases in funding must be targeted to important problems and attract the best researchers in the country to work on them. Thus, funding should increase as other design principles are institutionalized in a federal education research agency. In particular, steady growth in funding for research should occur as parallel investments are made in human resources in the agency and in the field of education research more globally, the topic we take up next.

DESIGN PRINCIPLE 6
Invest in Research Infrastructure

The infrastructure of any organization is the basic underlying system that determines how it functions to meet its mission. Research infrastructure includes a wide range of supports, but most commonly refers to scientists in the field (people), the tools those scientists have to conduct their work (instrumentation and methods), and the resources those scientists need (time, money, and access to research participants). We believe it is essential for a federal education research agency to consistently invest part of its annual appropriations in infrastructure-building programs.

Specifically, we believe funding is particularly critical in three areas: the education research community; data development, information sharing, and access; and links with the practice and policy communities.

Community of Education Researchers

A federal agency must play a role in nurturing the community of education researchers. The greater the field's capacity to conduct high-quality scientific research in education and to monitor and maintain high scientific standards, the greater is the likelihood the agency will succeed in its mission. Our focus, consistent with the theme of developing a scientific culture in the agency, is on nurturing scientific norms in the field as a whole.

Historians tracing the field of education research have noted its failure "...to develop a strong, self-regulating professional community" (Lagemann, 2000, p. ix) over a long period of time. We argue throughout this report that the role of the community of scientists in enforcing scientific principles and engaging in professional, skeptical debate about a reasonably well-defined corpus of scientific work is paramount to the success of the enterprise. The complexity of education, and the attendant scope of the research effort, has to date hindered the ability of groups of scholars to form such a community with common intellectual focus.

The organization of programs of research within a federal education research agency (see Design Principle 4 above) would provide a natural springboard for the development of such communities (see http://www.rand.org/multi/achievementforall). The strategic focus of such programs and the standing panels that guide them can provide a common language and set of goals to coalesce groups of peer investigators. In addition, the agency should create incentives for those whom it funds to publish their research and syntheses in peer-reviewed journals.[8] Such incentives might include a requirement for progress reports to include evidence of peer-reviewed journal publications, final reports to be in the form of a series of journal articles, and evaluations of new proposals that take into

---

[8]Such journals typically demand, for example, justification of research questions based on balanced, critical reviews of prior research, use of rigorous methods and analyses, and a careful chain of logic in interpretations of findings.

consideration the publication record of the principal investigator and other key personnel.

A federal education research agency cannot develop and maintain these communities alone. It can leverage its investment in human resources through partnerships with other federal agencies, scholarly professional associations, colleges and universities (especially schools of education), journal publishers, and others. These partnerships could lay the foundation for broad-based efforts aimed at various parts of the system that interact with the education research profession. For example, partnerships with journal publishers and professional associations could lead to the development and monitoring of standards for journal publications and professional meetings. Collaborations with professional associations might feature training and fellowship programs for young scholars (e.g., the Statistics Institute at the annual meeting of the American Educational Research Association [AERA], funded jointly by OERI and the National Center for Education Statistics [NCES], or the AERA Research Grants Program funded by NSF, OERI, NCES, and AERA [Shavelson, 1991] to support dissertation and field-initiated research studies and to place research fellows at NSF and NCES). The agency could also forge links with schools of education, schools of arts and sciences, and other university departments to develop strategies for training and supporting future scientists in education research.

The training of education researchers is a long-term undertaking. As we discuss in Chapter 1, current scholarship in education is generated by investigators trained in schools of education as well as in, for example, psychology, history, economics, sociology, mathematics, biology, and public policy departments. In schools of education, students often pursue nonresearch-oriented goals (e.g., school administration) and may therefore reach the graduate level without any research training. In a related vein, publication standards and peer review also vary considerably in education journals. These complex structural issues will require careful study and innovative approaches to address them effectively.

Data Development, Sharing, and Access

The advancement of scientific knowledge is facilitated when investigators work with the same set of variables and theoretical constructs. Ideally, the field uses a common set of constructs across research studies to enable replication in different contexts and to better understand the extent to which findings from one study can be extended in other situations. This common core would facilitate understanding of how variables and relationships between variables change over time; if the construct changes, there is no basis for comparison from one time to another. In education, this base has been difficult to establish. As we argue in Chapter 4, there is little consensus about the goals of education, which has presented the community with the challenge of making sense of findings from multiple studies on similar topics but based on different measures. Weak theoretical understanding (see Chapter 5) is another reason why such constructs have not yet been fully developed in education.

A federal education research agency is a logical central place to develop and maintain databases that house these common variables. With the emergence of new technologies for data collection, management, and analysis, such an agency, perhaps in collaboration with an education statistics agency (like the current NCES) and as theory is strengthened, could develop the capacity to maintain data systems on major issues that provide rich information about educational achievement, processes, costs, institutions, policies, and services on an ongoing basis. The system could draw on the extensive resources already available through NCES, the Organisation for Economic Co-operation and Development (OECD), and NSF and develop a system based on a common conceptual frame that links these data in a coherent way.[9] For similar reasons, the agency should encourage and facilitate data sharing among its grantees while ensuring privacy and other ethical standards are met.

A key role for a federal education research agency in developing the data infrastructure for scientific education research is by facilitating access to research participants (e.g., students, teachers, administrators, policy makers) and sites (e.g., classrooms, schools, state legislatures). This access is essential to the viability of education research and its potential as a tool for improv-

---

[9]The committee is aware that similar efforts in the past have failed. The development of a conceptual framework will be difficult and contentious, but the lack of coherence across existing indicator systems is a serious problem in education research and should continue to be pursued as a long-term goal.

ing education, but researchers have difficulty gaining access to these sources of data for at least two reasons. First, educational practitioners (especially teachers) typically do not see education research as useful to their day-to-day work (Weiss, 1995). This indifference often means that school officials are unwilling to commit the resources (which is usually a substantial amount of time) required to engage in research efforts. A second reason arises out of federal rules and regulations regarding research ethics. Data access for education research involves legitimate concerns about protecting research participants—particularly young students—from inappropriate actions in the name of research. Protections for human research participants, including participants in education research, have been in effect in the United States since 1974 (now codified in Title 45 Part 46 of the U.S. Code of Federal Regulations). The primary protective mechanism outlined in these federal regulations are institutional review boards (IRBs), oversight groups that review all federally funded research involving human participants to ensure their ethical treatment.

It is important to recognize that education research, including evaluation studies, rarely presents any true risk to the participant so long as care is taken to protect identities and that researchers understand and are responsive to the needs of individual participants. Explicit exemptions outlined in the U.S. code (see Box 6-1) make this clear. Tom Puglisi, the former Director of Human Subject Protections in the federal Office for Human Research Protections, summed up the intent of current law most succinctly by stating that "much social and behavioral research is exempt from the regulations governing research" (Puglisi, 2001, p. 34).

In addition to this core statute, there are at least two other laws (the Family Education Rights and Privacy Act and the Protection of Pupil Rights Amendment) and U.S. Department of Education policy (developed by the agency's Family Policy Compliance Office) that govern access to education data. In combination, these rules have been variously interpreted and implemented, often creating confusion and erecting unnecessary barriers to conducting scientific research that typically poses "minimal risk" to students. To add to this already maze-like array of statutes, regulations, and policies, a recently passed amendment (Parental Freedom of Information Amendment) to the U.S. House of Representatives version of the pending "No Child Left Behind" legislation, would compound the situation further. Ironically, this amendment would undermine the $30 million evaluation program proposed in the same bill.

Research ethics is a complex area that the committee did not have the time nor the expertise to consider fully.[10] The committee believes that the basic principles that underlie these regulations and govern the ethical conduct of research involving human participants must be upheld; however, we do see bureaucratic problems and inconsistencies in the way these principles have been implemented. A federal education research agency will need to address these issues as a vital part of its investment in building infrastructure. If ethical access to data on students cannot be achieved, scientific progress will be seriously hindered. We suggest that the agency, in collaboration with other federal agencies conducting science-based education research and other interested groups (e.g., social science research associations, research ethicists) invest some of its resources to work toward the dual goals of scientific access to data and protection of individuals. Without ethical access to research participants and sites, the mission of the agency cannot be met.

Links to Practice and Policy Communities

We argue above that the practice and policy communities must be engaged in the work of the agency to develop its research agenda. We also call for regular syntheses of research findings to inform practitioners and policy makers about the cumulative knowledge that scientific education research has generated. Here, we suggest a third connection to practice and policy communities, based on the premise that field-based education research that adheres to scientific principles (see Chapter 3) and attends to the features of education (see Chapter 4) will be significantly strengthened by an infrastructure that bridges the gap between researchers and practitioners.

We wish to be clear that we are not calling for the agency to develop a dissemination network to "translate" research into practice. The transla-

---

[10]The National Research Council's Panel on Institutional Review Boards, Surveys, and Social Science Research is reviewing current and proposed methods of human subjects' protection in social science data collection. It is focusing on the structure, function, and performance of the institutional review board system.

tion of research findings into practice is not a straightforward affair, and indeed, many have rejected this common metaphor outright (see e.g., Willinsky, 2001). The effect of social science on practice is typically indirect, affecting change incrementally through "knowledge creep" (Weiss, 1980, 1991a, 1999). The scholarly literature on research utilization also suggests that local application of knowledge is a long-term process that involves changes in practitioners' beliefs, as well as in their procedural skill for implementing the knowledge (Weiss, 1991b, 1999). And how to spark exempt under paragraph (b)(2) of this section, if: (i) the human subjects are elected or appointed public officials or candidates for public office; or (ii) federal statute(s) require(s) without exception that the confidentiality of the personally identifiable information will be maintained throughout the research and thereafter.

(4) Research, involving the collection or study of existing data, documents, records, pathological specimens, or diagnostic specimens, if these sources are publicly available or if the information is recorded by the investigator in such a manner that subjects cannot be identified, directly or through identifiers linked to the subjects.

(5) Research and demonstration projects which are conducted by or subject to the approval of department or agency heads, and which are designed to study, evaluate, or otherwise examine: (i) public benefit or service programs; (ii) procedures for obtaining benefits or services under those programs; (iii) possible changes in or alternatives to those programs or procedures; or (iv) possible changes in methods or levels of payment for benefits or services under those programs.

SOURCE: Code of Federal Regulations. Title 45-Public Welfare, Part 46-Protection of Human Subjects, pp. 107-108. Washington, DC: U.S. Government Printing Office.

large-scale change in the U.S. education system—research-based or otherwise—is not well understood (Elmore, 1996).

Two recent reports have drawn on these and related literatures to suggest fundamentally new ways of organizing the education research enterprise. The first, *Improving Student Learning: A Strategic Plan for Education Research and Its Utilization* (National Research Council, 1999d), makes the case that education research would have a stronger impact on practice if it were supported by an infrastructure that promoted ongoing collaborations among researchers, practitioners, and policy makers. A second phase of this Strategic Education Research Partnership is currently focused on how to take this idea and build a place—and the enabling strategies, incentives, and infrastructure—to allow these partnerships to flourish. The second, a report of the National Academy of Education (1999), made a similar argument that the prevailing model of research implementation—moving from basic research to development to large-scale implementation of programs—is based on simplistic assumptions about the nature of education and education research. The report concluded that a more productive perspective would view research production and research understanding as part of the same process, also suggesting the need for better partnerships between researchers and educators. Both reports, therefore, simultaneously urge the supply of, and the demand for, education research.

Although the critical issue of research utilization is beyond the scope of the committee's charge (although we do believe that more research on the topic is very much needed), we focus here on the benefits to scientific inquiry that these collaborative models envision. We suggest that a federal education research agency invest in an infrastructure that builds connections between researchers and practitioners because we see the potential to enhance the research itself. Sustained collaborations between researchers and practitioners could strengthen field-based scientific education research by incrementally infusing a deeper knowledge of the complexities of educational practice into theory building, empirical testing, and methods development in a number of ways. First, situating the research in the messiness of day-to-day educational environments would enable closer attention to context, which we argue is essential to recognize and treat in scientific research. This infrastructure would also establish mutual trust and working relationships that could offer long-term, facilitated access to research participants and sites, and so protect against research being abandoned (as we describe in Chapter 4) when the dynamic conditions surrounding education inevitably shift (e.g., changes in school leadership). Furthermore, strategically and appropriately engaging the knowledge of practitioners' craft throughout the research process can provide relevant insights that otherwise might be missed.

There are a few examples of such models in practice (e.g., Consortium on Chicago School Reform, http://www.consortium-chicago.org), but this kind of infrastructure building is fundamentally new. We suggest that an agency support such partnerships carefully and incrementally. There are not only significant structural and cultural barriers to forging these partnerships, but there is also the potential for them to be unproductive. The nature of their work requires practitioners to be driven by immediate crises of the day. These needs could skew the research to be too short-term and tactical in nature to contribute substantially to science-based knowledge. Similarly, there may also be tradeoffs between traditional views of scientific quality and the utility of the work for practice (National Research Council, 2001d). Thus, we urge that the development of these collaborations should include explicit plans for studying their effectiveness and improving them over time.

CONCLUSION

We believe that clear and consistent focus on translating these design principles into action will promote a strong scientific culture within an agency and strengthen the federal role in education research. For those who know the history of NIE or OERI, many of the principles will strike a familiar chord. For those who don't, many of them will seem self-evident. However hackneyed or intuitive, we believe they are the crux of the matter. Too often "reform" efforts of the past have focused on changing the existing agency's organizational structure without adequately grappling with the core issues related to building an infrastructure that supports a scientific community and fosters scientific norms within the agency. Arguably, not since the early days of NIE has the primary agency in the federal government charged with education research had the basic tools to develop a scientific culture and to achieve its mission. Although the details may shift, the principles we propose are intended to stand as guideposts for a federal agency charged with support of scientific education research regardless of the particular situation of the existing federal infrastructure at any given point in time.

References

Achilles, C. (1999). *Let's put kids first, finally: Getting class size right.* Thousand Oaks, CA: Corwin Press.

Adams, M.J. (1990). *Beginning to read: Thinking and learning about print.* Cambridge, MA: MIT Press.

Agar, M. (1996). *The professional stranger: An informal introduction to ethnography.* San Diego: Academic Press.

Alberts, B., Bray, D., Johnson, A., Lewis, J., Walter, P., Roberts, K., and Raff, M. (1997). *Essential cell biology: An introduction to the molecular biology of the cell.* New York: Garland.

Altonji, J.G. (1988). The effects of family background and school characteristics on education and labor market outcomes. Unpublished manuscript, Northwestern University, Evanston, IL.

American Educational Research Association. (2000). *Creating knowledge in the 21st century: Insights from multiple perspectives.* 2000 Annual Meeting Program. Washington, DC: Author.

August, D., and Muraskin, L. (1999). Strengthening the standards: Recommendations for OERI peer review. Summary report. Prepared for the National Educational Research Policy and Priorities Board, U.S. Department of Education.

Ball, D.L., and Lampert, M. (1999). Multiples of evidence, time, and perspective: Revising the study of teaching and learning. In E.C. Lagemann and L. Shulman (Eds.), *Issues in education research.* San Francisco: Jossey-Bass.

Bane, M.J. (2001). Presidential address. Expertise, advocacy, and deliberation: Lessons from welfare reform. *Journal of Policy Analysis and Management, 20*(2), 191-197.

Barnard, J., Frangakis, C., Hill, J., and Rubin, D. (2002). Bayesian analysis of the New York School Choice Scholarships Program: A randomized experiment with noncompliance and missing data. In C. Gatsonis, R.E. Cass, B. Carlin, A. Carriquiry, A. Gelman, I. Verdinelli, and M. West (Eds.), *Case studies in Bayesian statistics*. New York: Springer-Verlag.

Baumeister, R.F., Bratslavsky, E., Muraven, M., and Tice, D.M. (1998). Ego depletion: Is the active self a limited resource? *Journal of Personality and Social Psychology, 74*(5), 1252-1265.

Beardslee, W.R., Wright, E.J., Salt, P., and Drezner, K. (1997). Examination of children's responses to two preventive intervention strategies over time. *Journal of the American Academy of Child & Adolescent Psychiatry, 36*(2), 196-204.

Behr, M.J., Lesh, R., Post, T.R., and Silver, E.A. (1983). Rational number concepts. In R. Lesh and M. Landau (Eds.), *Acquisition of mathematics concepts and processes* (pp. 91-125). New York: Academic Press.

Berger, A., Imbrie, J., Hays, J., Kukla, G., and Saltzman, B. (Eds.). (1984). *Milankovitch and climate*. Hingham, MA: D. Reidel.

Betts, J. (1995). Does school quality matter? Evidence from the national longitudinal survey of youth. *Review of Economics and Statistics, 77,* 231-247.

Blachman, B.A. (2000). Phonological awareness. In M.L. Kamil, P.B. Mosenthal, P.D. Pearson, and R. Barr (Eds.), *Handbook of reading research: Vol. III* (pp. 483-502). Mahwah, NJ: Lawrence Erlbaum Associates.

Blumer, H. (1966). Foreword. In S. Bruyn (Ed.), *The human perspective in sociology: The methodology of participant observation* (pp. iii-vii). Englewood Cliffs, NJ: Prentice-Hall.

Bogatz, G.A., and Ball, S. (1972). *The impact of Sesame Street on children's first school experiences*. Children's Television Workshop, New York, NY. [BBB03935], Educational Testing Service, Princeton, NJ [QAT24225].

Bohrnstedt, G.W., and Stecher, B.M. (1999). *Class size reduction in California 1996-1998: Early findings signal promise and concerns*. Palo Alto, CA: CSR Research Consortium, American Institutes for Research.

Boruch, R.F. (1997). *Randomized experiments for planning and evaluation: A practical guide*. Thousand Oaks, CA: Sage.

Boruch, R.F., DeMoya, D., and Snyder, B. (in press). The importance of randomized field trials in education and related areas. In F. Mosteller and R. Boruch (Eds.), *Evidence matters: Randomized trials in education research*. Washington, DC: Brookings Institution Press.

Boruch, R.F., and Foley, E. (2000). The honestly experimental society: Sites and other entities as the units of allocation and analysis in randomized trials. In L. Bickman (Ed.), *Validity and experimentation: Donald Campbell's legacy* (pp. 193-238). Thousand Oaks, CA: Sage.

Boruch, R.F., Snyder, B., and DeMoya, D. (2000). The importance of randomized field trials. *Crime and Delinquency, 46*(2), 156-180.

Broeker, W.S. (1992). Climate cycles: Upset for Milankovitch theory. *Nature, 359*, 779-780.

Brooks, H. (1967). Applied science and technological progress. *Science, 156*, 1706-1712.

Brophy, J.E., and Good, T.L. (1986). Teacher behavior and student achievement. In M.C. Wittrock (Ed.), *Handbook of research on teaching* (3rd ed., pp 328-375). New York: Macmillan.

Brown, A.L. (1992). Design experiments: Theoretical and methodological challenges in creating complex interventions in classroom settings. *Journal of the Learning Sciences, 2*(2), 141-178.

Brown, W. (1910). Some experimental results in the correlation of mental abilities. *British Journal of Psychology, 3*, 296-322.

Bruner, J. (1996). *The culture of education.* Cambridge, MA: Harvard University Press.

Bryk, A.S., Lee, V.A., and Holland, P.B. (1993). *Catholic schools and the common good.* Cambridge, MA: Harvard University Press.

Bryk, A.S., and Raudenbush, S.W. (1988). Toward a more appropriate conceptualization of research on school effects: A three-level linear model. *American Journal of Education, 97*(1), 65-108.

Bryk, A.S., Sebring, P.B., Kerbow, D., Rollow, S., and Easton, J.Q. (1998). *Charting Chicago school reform: Democratic localism as a lever for change.* Boulder, CO: Westview Press.

Burtless, G. (Ed.). (1996). *Does money matter? The effect of school resources on student achievement and adult success.* Washington, DC: Brookings Institution Press.

Burtless, G. (in press). Randomized field trials for policy evaluation: Why not in education? In F. Mosteller and R. Boruch (Eds.), *Evidence matters: Randomized trials in education research.* Washington, DC: Brookings Institution Press.

Campbell, D.T. (1957). Factors relevant to the validity of experiments in social settings. *Psychological Bulletin, 54(4),* 297-312.

Campbell, D.T. (1969). Reforms as experiments. *American Psychologist, 24*(4), 409-429.

Campbell, D.T., and Stanley, J.C. (1963). Experimental and quasi-experimental designs for research on teaching. In N.L. Gage (Ed.), *Handbook of research on teaching* (pp. 171-246). Washington, DC: American Educational Research Association. (Printed by Rand McNally & Company).

Caporoso, J.A., and Roos, L.L., Jr. (1973). *Quasi-experimental approaches: Testing theory and evaluating policy*. Evanston, IL: Northwestern University Press.

Carr, E.G., Levin, L., McConnachie, G., Carlson, J.I., Kemp, D.C., Smith, C.E., and McLaughlin, D.M. (1999). Comprehensive multisituational intervention for problem behavior in the community: Long-term maintenance and social validation. *Journal of Positive Behavior Interventions, 1*(1), 5-25.

Carroll, J.B. (1993). *Human cognitive abilities: A survey of factor-analytic studies.* Cambridge, England: Cambridge University Press.

Chall, J. (1967). *Learning to read: The great debate.* New York: McGraw-Hill.

Chubin, D.E., and Hackett, E.J. (1990). *Peerless science: Peer review and U.S. science policy.* Albany, NY: State University of New York Press.

Cichetti, D.V. (1991). The reliability of peer review for manuscript and grant submissions: A cross-disciplinary investigation. *Behavioral and Brain Sciences, 14*(1), 119-135.

Cochran. W.G. (1983). *Planning and analysis of observational studies.* New York: Wiley.

Cohen, D.K., Raudenbush, S.W., and Ball, D.L. (in press). Resources, instruction, and research. In F. Mosteller and R. Boruch (Eds.), *Evidence matters: Randomized trials in education research.* Washington, DC: Brookings Institution Press.

Cohn, V. (1989). *News and numbers: A guide to reporting statistical claims and controversies in health and other fields.* Ames, IA: Iowa State University Press.

Coleman, J.S., Cambell, E. Q., Hobson, C. F., McPartland, J., Mood, A. M., Weinfeld, F. D., and York, R. L. (1966). *Equality of educational opportunity.* Washington, DC: U.S. Government Printing Office.

Coleman, J.S., Hoffer, T., and Kilgore, S. (1982). *High school achievement: Public, Catholic, and other private schools compared.* New York: Basic Books.

Confrey, J., and Lachance, A. (2000). Transformative teaching experiments through conjecture-driven research design. In A. E. Kelly and R. A. Lesh (Eds.), *Handbook of research design in mathematics and science education* (pp. 17-34). Mahwah, NJ: Lawrence Erlbaum Associates.

Cook, R., Lawrence, H., Morse, C., and Roehl, J.A. (1984). An evaluation of the alternatives approach to drug abuse prevention. *International Journal of the Addictions, 19*(7), 767-787.

Cook, T.D. (2001). Sciencephobia. *Education Next, 1*(3), 62-68.

Cook, T.D., and Campbell, D.T. (Eds). (1979). *Quasi-experimentation: Design and analysis issues for field settings.* Boston, MA: Houghton Mifflin.

Cook, T.D., and Campbell, D.T. (1986). The causal assumptions of quasi-experimental practice. *Synthese, 68*(1), 141-180.

Cook, T.D., and Payne, M.R. (in press). Objecting to the objections to using random assignment in educational research. In F. Mosteller and R. Boruch (Eds.), *Evidence matters: Randomized trials in education research.* Washington, DC: Brookings Institution Press.

Cooper, H., and Hedges, L.V. (Eds.). (1994). *Handbook of research synthesis.* New York: Russell Sage Foundation.

Crawford, J. (1992). *Hold your tongue: Bilingualism and the politics of "English only."* Reading, MA: Addison-Wesley.

Cremin, L. (1990). *Popular education and its discontents.* New York: Harper & Row.

Cronbach, L.J. (1951). Coefficient alpha and the internal structure of tests. *Psychometrika, 16*(3), 297-334.

Cronbach, L.J. (1971). Test validation. In R.L. Thorndike (Ed.), *Educational measurement,* 2nd ed (pp. 443-508). Washington, DC: American Council on Education.

Cronbach, L.J. (1975). Beyond the two disciplines of scientific psychology. *American Psychologist, 30,* 671-684.

Cronbach, L.J. (with Shapiro, K.). (1982). *Designing evaluations of educational and social programs.* San Francisco: Jossey-Bass.

Cronbach, L.J. (1989). Lee J. Cronbach. In G. Lindzey (Ed.), *A history of psychology in autobiography:* Vol. VIII, (pp. 64-93). Stanford, CA: Stanford University Press.

Cronbach, L.J., Ambron, S.R., Dornbusch, S.M., Hess, R.D., Hornik, R.C., Phillips, D.C., Walker, D.F., and Weiner, S.S. (1980). *Toward reform of program evaluation.* San Francisco: Jossey Bass.

Cronbach, L.J., Gleser, G.C., Nanda, H., and Rajaratnam, N. (1972). *The dependability of behavioral measurements: Theory of generalizability for scores and profiles.* New York: Wiley.

Cronbach, L.J., Rajaratnam, N., and Gleser, G.C. (1963). Theory of generalizability: A liberalization of reliability theory. *British Journal of Statistical Psychology, 16,* 137-163.

Cronbach, L.J., and Suppes, P. (Eds.). (1969). *Research for tomorrow's schools.* New York: Macmillan.

Day, J.C. (1996). *Population projections of the United States by age, sex, race, and Hispanic origin: 1995 to 2050.* U.S. Bureau of the Census, Current Population Reports, P25-1130. Washington, DC: U.S. Government Printing Office.

Day, J., and Kalman, D. (2001). Teaching linear algebra: Issues and resources. *The College Mathematics Journal, 32*(3), 162-168.

deNeufville, J.I. (1975). *Social indicators and public policy: Interactive processes of design and application.* New York: Elsevier.

Denzin, N. (1978). *The research act: A theoretical introduction to sociological methods.* New York: McGraw-Hill.

Derry, G.N. (1999). *What science is and how it works.* Princeton, NJ: Princeton University Press.

Dewey, J. (1916). *Democracy and education.* New York: Macmillan.

Dewey, J. (1929). *The sources of a science of education.* New York: Livewright.

Dewey, J. (1938). *Logic: The theory of inquiry.* New York: H. Holt and Company.

Diamond, J. (1999). *Guns, germs, and steel.* New York: W.W. Norton and Company.

Donner, A., and Klahr, N. (2000). *Design and analysis of cluster randomization trials in health research.* London: Arnold.

Du Bois, P.H. (1970) *A history of psychological testing.* Boston: Allyn and Bacon.

Duneier, M. (1999). *Sidewalk.* New York: Farrar, Straus and Giroux.

Eden, G.F., and Zeffiro, T.A. (1998). Neural systems affected in developmental dyslexia revealed by functional neuroimaging. *Neuron, 21*(2), 279-282.

Edgeworth, F.Y. (1888). The statistics of examinations. *Journal of the Royal Statistical Society, 51*, 599-635.

Edmonds, R. (1984). School effects and teacher effects. *Social Policy, 15*(2), 37-39.

Ehrenberg, R.G., and Brewer, D.J. (1994). Do school and teacher characteristics matter? Evidence from high school and beyond. *Economics of Education Review, 13*, 1-17.

Einstein, A., and Infeld, L. (1938). *The evolution of physics.* New York: Simon and Schuster.

Eisner, E.W. (1991). *The enlightened eye: Qualitative inquiry and the enhancement of educational practice.* New York: Macmillan.

Elmore, R.F. (1996). Getting to scale with good educational practice. *Harvard Educational Review, 66*(1), 1-26.

Farley, K.A. (1995). Cenozoic variations in the flux of interplanetary dust recorded by sup 3He in a deep-sea sediment. *Nature, 376*, 153-156.

Feldman, M., and March, J.G. (1981). Information in organizations as signal and symbol. *Administrative Science Quarterly, 26*, 171-186.

Feng, Y., and Vasconcelos, P. (2001). Quaternary continental weathering geochronology by laser-heating 40Ar/39Ar analysis of supergene cryptomelane. *Geology, 29*(7), 635-638.

Ferguson, R.F. (1991). Paying for public education: New evidence on how and why money matters. *Harvard Journal on Legislation, 28*, 465-98.

Finn, C., Jr. (2001). Trouble ahead? *Philanthropy, 15*(3), 36-37.

Finn, J.D., and Achilles, C.M. (1990). Answers and questions about class size: A statewide experiment. *American Educational Research Journal, 27*(3), 557-577.

Finn, J.D., and Achilles, C.M. (1999). Tennessee's Class Size Study: Findings, Implications, Misconceptions. *Educational Evaluation and Policy Analysis, 21*(2), 97-109.

Fletcher, J.M., and Lyon, G.R. (1998). Reading: A research-based approach. In W. Evers (Ed.), *What's gone wrong in America's classrooms* (pp. 49-90). Stanford, CA: Hoover Institution Press.

Folger, J., and Breda, C. (1989). Evidence from Project STAR about class size and student achievement. *Peabody Journal of Education 67*(1), 17-33.

Forgione, P.D. (2001). Testimony to the U.S. House Committee on Education and the Workforce. 107th Cong., 1st Sess.

Fuchs, L.S., Fuchs, D., and Kazdan, S. (1999). Effects of peer-assisted learning strategies on high school students with serious reading problems. *Remedial & Special Education, 20*(5), 309-318.

Fuhrman, S. (2001). The policy influence of education R&D centers. Testimony to The U.S. House Committee on Education and the Workforce. 107th Cong., 1st Sess.

Garcia, E.E., and Wiese, A. (In press). Language, public policy and schooling: A focus on Chicano English language learners. In R. Valencia (Ed.), *Chicano school failure and success (2nd ed.)*. New York: The Falmer Press.

Geweke, J., and Straf, M. (1999). Principles for managing social-science research in government. Paper presented to the National Research Council Committee on National Statistics, May 7, 1999.

Gibbs, W.W. (2001). Shrinking to enormity. *Scientific American, 284*, 33-34.

Gibson, E.J., and Levin, H. (1975). *The psychology of reading*. Cambridge, MA: MIT Press.

Glass, G.V., Cahen, L.S., Smith, M.L., and Filby, N.N. (1982). *School class size: Research and policy*. Beverly Hills, CA: Sage.

Glass, G.V., and Smith, M.L. (1978). *Meta-analysis of research on the relationship of class size and achievement*. San Francisco: Far West Laboratory of Educational Research and Development.

Goldberger, A.S. (1972). Selection bias in evaluating treatment effects. Discussion Paper No. 123-172. Institute for Research on Poverty, University of Wisconsin, Madison.

Goldberger, A.S. (1983). Abnormal selection bias. In S. Karlin, T. Amemiya, and L.A. Goodman (Eds.), *Studies in econometrics, time series, and multivariate statistics: In honor of Theodore W. Anderson* (pp. 67-84). New York: Academic Press.

Gorman, C.A., Garrity, J.A., Fatoourecchi, V., Bahn, R.S., Petersen, I.A., Stafford, S.L., Earle, J.D., Forbes, G.S., Kline, R.W., Bergstralh, E.J., Offord, K.P., Rademacher, D.M., Stanley, N.M., and Bartley, G.B. (2001). A prospective, randomized, double-blind, placebo-controlled study of orbital radiotherapy for Graves' ophthalmopathy. *Ophthalmology, 108*(9), 1523-1534.

Greeley, A.M. (1982). *Catholic high schools and minority students.* New Brunswick, NJ: Transaction Books.

Greeno, J.G., Collins, A.M., and Resnick, L.B. (1996). Cognition and learning. In D. C. Berliner and R. C. Calfee (Eds.), *Handbook of educational psychology* (pp. 15-46). New York: Simon & Schuster Macmillan.

Grigorenko, E.L. (1999). The biological foundations of developmental dyslexia. In R.J. Sternberg and L. Spear-Swerling (Eds.), *Perspectives on learning disabilities* (pp. 3-22). Oxford: Westview Press.

Grissmer, D. (Ed.). (1999). Class size: Issues and new findings [Special issue]. *Educational Evaluation and Policy Analysis, 21*(2).

Grissmer, D.W., and Flanagan, A. (2000). Moving educational research toward scientific consensus. In D. W. Grissmer and J. M. Ross (Eds.), *Analytic issues in the assessment of student achievement.* Washington, DC: U.S. Department of Education, National Center for Education Statistics.

Grogger, J. (1996). School expenditures and post-schooling earnings: Evidence from high school and beyond. *The Review of Economics and Statistics, 78,* 628-637.

Gross, P.R., Levitt, N., and Lewis, M. (1997). *The flight from science and reason.* New York: New York Academy of Sciences.

Grossman, D. (2001). Profile: Astrophysicist Richard A. Muller. *Scientific American, 284,* 30-32.

Guba, E.G., and Lincoln, Y.S. (1981). *Effective evaluation.* San Francisco: Jossey-Bass.

Guilford, J.P. (1967). *The nature of human intelligence.* New York: McGraw-Hill.

Gulliksen, H. (1950a). History of and present trends in testing. Research Memorandum RM-50-32, Princeton, NJ: Educational Testing Service.

Gulliksen, H. (1950b). *Theory of mental tests.* New York: John Wiley.

Gustasson, J-E, and Undheim, J.O. (1996). Individual differences in cognitive functions. In D.C. Berliner and R.C. Calfee (Eds.), *Handbook of educational psychology* (pp. 186-242). New York: Macmillan.

Guttman, L. (1953). A special review of Harold Gulliksen, *Theory of mental tests. Psychometrika, 18,* 123-130.

Hanushek, E.A. (1981). Throwing money at schools. *Journal of Policy Analysis & Management, 1*(1), 19-41.

Hanushek, E.A. (1986). The economics of schooling: Production and efficiency in public schools. *Journal of Economic Literature, 24,* 1141-1177.

Hanushek, E.A. (1997). Assessing the effects of school resources on student performance: An update. *Educational Evaluation & Policy Analysis, 19,* 141-164.

Hanushek, E.A. (1999a). The evidence on class size. In S.E. Mayer and P. Peterson (Eds.), *Earning and learning: How schools matter* (pp. 131-168). Washington, DC: Brookings Institution Press.

Hanushek, E.A. (1999b). Some findings from an independent investigation of the Tennessee STAR experiment and from other investigations of class size effects. *Educational Evaluation and Policy Analysis, 21*(2), 143-164

Hanushek, E.A., Kain, J.F., and Rivkin, S.G. (1998, August). Teachers, schools and academic achievement. NBER Working Paper W6691. Cambridge, MA: National Bureau of Economic Research.

Harel, G., and Confrey, J. (Eds.). (1994). *The development of multiplicative reasoning in the learning of mathematics.* Albany, NY: SUNY Press.

Heckman, J.J. (1979). Sample selection bias as a specification error. *Econometrica, 47,* 153-161.

Heckman, J.J. (1980a). Addendum to 'Sample Selection Bias as a Specification Error.' In E.W. Stromsdorfer and G. Farkas (Eds.), *Evaluation studies: Review annual:*Vol. 5 (pp. 69-74). Beverly Hills, CA: Sage.

Heckman, J.J. (1980b). Sample selection bias as a specification error with an application to the estimation of labor supply functions. In J.P. Smith (Ed.), *Female labor supply: Theory and estimation* (pp.206-248). Princeton, NJ: Princeton University Press.

Heckman, J.J. (2001). Micro data, heterogeneity, and the evaluation of public policy: Nobel Lecture. *Journal of Political Economy, 109*(4), 673-748.

Hedges, L.V., Laine, R.D., and Greenwald, R. (1994). Does money matter? A meta-analysis of studies of the effects of differential school inputs on student outcomes. *Educational Researcher* 23(3), 5-14.

Hedges, L.V., and Olkin, I. (1983). Regression models in research synthesis. *American Statistician, 37,* 137-140.

Hirst, P.H., and Peters, R.S. (1970). *The logic of education.* London: Routledge.

Holland, D.C., and Eisenhart, M.A. (1990). *Educated in romance: Women, achievement, and college culture.* Chicago. University of Chicago Press.

Holland, P.W. (1993). Which comes first, cause or effect? In G. Keren, and C. Lewis (Eds.), *A handbook for data analysis in the behavioral sciences: Methodological issues* (pp. 273-282). Hillsdale, NJ: Lawrence Erlbaum Associates.

Howe, K. (1988). Against the quantitative-qualitative incompatibility thesis. *Educational Research, 17*(8), 10-16.

Howe, K., and Eisenhart, M. (1990). Standards for qualitative (and quantitative) research: A prolegomenon. *Educational Researcher, 19*(4), 2-9.

Hruz, T. (2000). The costs and benefits of smaller classes in Wisconsin: A further evaluation of the SAGE program. *Wisconsin Policy Research Institute Report, 13*(6).

Jackson, A. (1996). New directions at the IAS. *Notices of the American Mathematical Society, 43*(11), 1359-1362.

Jencks, C., Smith, M., Acland, H., Bane, M.J., Cohen, D., Gintis, H., Heyns, B., and Michelson, S. (1972). *Inequality: A reassessment of the effect of family and schooling in America.* New York: Basic Books.

Judy, R.W., and D'Amico, C. (1997). *Workforce 2020: Work and workers in the 21st century.* Indianapolis: Hudson Institute.

Kaestle, C.F. (1993). The awful reputation of education research. *Educational Researcher, 22*(1), 26-31.

Karner, D.B., and Muller, R.A. (2000). A causality problem for Milankovitch. *Science, 288,* 2143-2144.

Kelley, T.L. (1923). *Statistical method.* New York: Macmillan.

Kelly, A.E., and Lesh, R.A., (Eds.). (2000). *Handbook of research design in mathematics and science education.* Mahwah, NJ: Lawrence Erlbaum Associates.

Kelly, A.E., and Lesh, R.A. (2000). Trends and shifts in research methods. In A. E. Kelly and R.A. Lesh, (Eds.), *Handbook of research design in mathematics and science education* (pp. 35-44). Mahwah, NJ: Lawrence Erlbaum Associates.

King, G., Keohane, R., and Verba, S. (1994). *Designing social inquiry: Scientific inference in qualitative research.* Princeton: Princeton University Press.

Kirst, M.W., and Mazzeo, C. (1996). The rise, fall, and rise of state assessment in California, 1993-96. *Phi Delta Kappan 78*(4), 319-323.

Krathwohl, D.R. (1998). *Methods of educational and social science research: An integrated approach.* New York: Longman.

Krueger, A.B. (1999). Experimental estimates of education production functions. *Quarterly Journal of Economics, CXIV,* 497-532.

Krueger, A.B., and Whitmore, D.M. (2001). The effect of attending a small class in the early grades on college-test taking and middle school test results: Evidence from Project STAR. *Economic Journal, 111,* 1-28.

Krueger, F., and Spearman, C. (1907). Die korrelation zwischen verschiedenen geistigen leistungfahigkeiten. *Zeitschrift fur Psychologie, 44,* 50-114.

Kuder, G.F., and Richardson, M.W. (1937) The theory of estimation of test reliability. *Psychometrika, 2,* 151-166.

Kuhn, T.S. (1962). *The structure of scientific revolutions.* Chicago: University of Chicago Press.

Lagemann, E.C. (1996). Contested terrain: A history of education research in the United States, 1890-1990. *Educational Researcher, 26*(9), 5.

Lagemann, E.C. (2000). *An elusive science: The troubling history of education research.* Chicago: University of Chicago Press.

Lakatos, I. (1970). Falsification and the methodology of scientific research programs. In I. Lakatos and A. Musgrave (Eds.), *Criticism and the growth of knowledge* (pp. 91-195). Cambridge, England: Cambridge University Press.

Lakatos, I., and Musgrave, A. (Eds.). (1970). *Criticism and the growth of knowledge.* Cambridge, England: Cambridge University Press.

Lambert, S.M., and Markel, H. (2000). Making history: Thomas Francis, Jr., M.D., and the 1954 Salk poliomyelitis vaccine field trial. *Archives of Pediatrics and Adolescent Medicine, 154*(5), 512-517.

Lawrence-Lightfoot, S. (1994). *I've known rivers: Lives of loss and liberation.* Reading, MA: Addison-Wesley.

Lawrence-Lightfoot, S., and Davis, J. H. (1997). *The art and science of portraiture.* San Francisco: Jossey-Bass.

Lesh, R.A, and Kelly, A.E. (2000). Multitiered teaching experiments. In A.E. Kelly and R.A. Lesh (Eds.), *Handbook of research design in mathematics and science education* (pp. 17-34). Mahwah, NJ: Lawrence Erlbaum Associates.

Lesh, R.A., Lovitts, B., and Kelly, A.E. (2000). Purposes and assumptions of this book. In A.E. Kelly and R.A. Lesh (Eds.), *Handbook of research design in mathematics and science education* (pp. 17-34). Mahwah, NJ: Lawrence Erlbaum Associates.

Levin, J.R., and O'Donnell, A.M. (1999). What to do about educational research's credibility gaps? *Issues in Education, 5*(2), 177-229.

Liberman, A.M. (1997). How theories of speech affect research in reading and writing. In B.A. Blachman (Ed.), *Foundations of reading acquisition and dyslexia: Implications for early intervention* (pp. 3-19). Mahwah, NJ: Lawrence Erlbaum Associates.

Liberman, A.L., Cooper, F.S., Shankweiler, D.P., and Studdert-Kennedy, M. (1967). Perception of the speech code. *Psychological Review, 74,* 731-761.

Liberman, I.Y. (1971). Basic research in speech and lateralization of language: Some implications for reading disability. *Bulletin of the Orton Society, 21,* 71-87.

Lindblom, C.E., and Cohen, D.K. (1979). *Usable knowledge: Social science and social problem solving.* New Haven: Yale University Press.

Lindblom, C.E., and Wodehouse, E.J. (1993). *The policy-making process* (3rd ed.). Englewood Cliffs, NJ: Prentice Hall.

Lock, S., and Wells, F. (1996). *Fraud and misconduct in medical research.* London: BMJ.

Loeb, S., and Page, M.E. (2000). Examining the link between teacher wages and student outcomes: The importance of alternative labor market opportunities and non-pecuniary variation. *Review of Economics & Statistics 82*(3), 393-408.

Lord, F.M. (1952). A theory of test scores. *Psychometric Monograph*, No. 7.

Lord, F.M., and Novick, M.R. (1968). *Statistical theories of mental test scores*. Reading, MA: Addison-Wesley.

MacDonald, G.J., and Sertorio, L. (Eds.). (1990). *Global climate and ecosystem change*. NATO ASI Series, Vol. B240. New York: Plenum Press.

Mack, N.K. (1990). Learning fractions with understanding: Building on informal knowledge. *Journal for Research in Mathematics Education, 21*(1), 16-32.

Mack, N.K. (1995). Confounding whole-number and fraction concepts when building on informal knowledge. *Journal for Research in Mathematics Education, 26*(5), 422-441.

Mackintosh, N.J. (Ed.). (1995). *Cyril Burt: Fraud or framed?* New York: Oxford University Press.

Mathtech. (1996). Comparison of selected federal R&D styles. Paper prepared for the National Educational Research Policy and Priorities Board, U.S. Department of Education.

Maxwell, J.A. (1996). *Qualitative research design: An interactive approach*. Thousand Oaks, CA: Sage.

Medical Research Council. (1948). Streptomycin treatment of pulmonary tuberculosis. *British Medical Journal, 2,* 769-782.

Merton, R.K. (1973). *The sociology of science: Theoretical and empirical investigations*. Chicago: University of Chicago Press.

Messick, S. (1989). Validity. In R.L. Linn (Ed.), *Educational measurement 3rd ed.,* (pp. 13-103). New York: Macmillan.

Messick, S. (1993). *Foundation of validity: Meaning and consequences in psychological assessment*. Princeton, NJ: Educational Testing Service.

Milankovitch, M. (1941/1969). *Canon of insolation of the Earth and its application to the problem of the ice ages* (Israel Program for Scientific Translations, Trans.). Jerusalem: Israel Program for Scientific Translations. (Original work published 1941). [Available from the National Technical Information Service: http://www.ntis.gov/]

Miles, M.B., and Huberman, A.M. (1994). *Qualitative data analysis: An expanded sourcebook*. Thousand Oaks, CA: Sage.

Miller, D.W. (2001, July 13). The problem with studying vouchers. *The Chronicle of Higher Education*, pp. A14-A15.

Mills, C.W. (2000). *The sociological imagination* (40th anniversary ed.). New York: Oxford University Press.

Mislevy, R.J. (1996). Test theory reconceived. *Journal of Educational Measurement, 33*(4), 379-416.

Mitchell, T.R., and Haro, A. (1999). Poles apart: Reconciling the dichotomies in education research. In E. C. Lagemann and L. Shulman (Eds.), *Issues in education research* (pp. 42-62). San Francisco: Jossey-Bass.

Morrill, W. (1998, October 6). Shaping the future of educational research, development, and communication. Working paper presented to the National Educational Research Policy and Priorities Board, U.S. Department of Education.

Moschkovich, J.N., and Brenner M.E. (2000). Integrating a naturalistic paradigm into research on mathematics and science cognition and learning. In A.E. Kelly and R.A. Lesh (Eds.), *Handbook of research design in mathematics and science education* (pp. 457-486). Mahwah, NJ: Lawrence Erlbaum Associates.

Moses, L.E. (1995). Measuring effects without randomized trials? Options, problems, challenges. *Medical Care, 33*(4, Suppl.), AS8-AS14.

Mosteller, F. (1995). The Tennessee study of class size in the early school grades. *The Future of Children, 5*(2), 113-127.

Mosteller, F., Gilbert, J.P., and McPeek, B. (1980). Reporting standards and research strategies for controlled trials: Agenda for the editor. *Controlled Clinical Trials, 1*, 37-58.

Muller, R.A. (1994). Glacial cycles and orbital inclination. Lawrence Berkeley Laboratory Report LBL-35665.

Murnane, R.J., and Levy, F. (1996). *Teaching the new basic skills: Principles for educating children to thrive in a changing economy.* New York: The Free Press.

Murnane, R.J., and Nelson, R. (1984). Production and innovation when techniques are tacit: The case of education. *Journal of Economic Behavior and Organizations, 5*, 353-373.

Murray, D.M. (1998). *Design and analysis of group randomized trials.* New York: Oxford University Press.

Murphy, E., Dingwall, R., Greatbatch, D., Parker, S., and Watson, P. (1998). Qualitative research methods in health technology assessment: A review of the literature. *Health Technology Assessment, 2*(16), vii-260.

Myers, D., Peterson, P., Mayer, D., Chou, J, and Howell, W.G. (2000). *School choice in New York City after two years: An evaluation of the school choice scholarships program. Interim Report.* Washington, DC: Mathematica Policy Research.

Myers, D., and Schirm, A. (1999). *The impacts of Upward Bound: Final report for phase I of the national evaluation.* Plainsboro, NJ: Mathematica Policy Research.

National Academy of Education. (1999). *Recommendations regarding research priorities: An advisory report to the National Educational Research Policy and Priorities Board.* New York: Author.

National Center for Education Statistics. (1996). *A descriptive summary of 1992-93 bachelor's degree recipients: 1 year later.* Washington, DC: U.S. Department of Education.

National Commission on Excellence in Education. (1983). *A nation at risk: The imperative for educational reform.* Washington, DC: U.S. Department of Education.

National Educational Research Policy and Priorities Board. (2000). *Investing in learning: A policy statement with recommendations on research in education. Investing in research: A second policy statement with further recommendations for research in education.* Washington, DC: U.S. Department of Education.

National Reading Panel. (2000). *Teaching children to read: An evidence-based assessment of the scientific research literature on reading and its implications for reading instruction.* Rockville, MD: National Institute of Child Health and Human Development.

National Research Council. (1958). *A proposed organization for research in education.* Washington, DC: National Academy of Sciences.

National Research Council. (1977). *Fundamental research and the process of education.* Committee on Fundamental Research Relevant to Education. S.B. Kiesler and C.F. Turner, Eds. Assembly of Behavioral and Social Sciences. Washington, DC: National Academy of Sciences.

National Research Council. (1986). *Creating a center for education statistics: A time for action.* Panel to Evaluate the National Center for Education Statistics. Committee on National Statistics. Commission on Behavioral and Social Sciences and Education. Washington, DC: National Academy Press.

National Research Council. (1991). *Performance assessment for the workplace: Vol. I.* Committee on the Performance of Military Personnel. Commission on Behavioral and Social Sciences and Education. Washington, DC: National Academy Press.

National Research Council. (1992). *Research and education reform: Roles for the Office of Educational Research and Improvement.* Committee on the Federal Role in Education Research. R.C. Atkinson and G.B. Jackson, Eds. Commission on Behavioral and Social Sciences and Education. Washington, DC: National Academy Press.

National Research Council. (1998). *Preventing reading difficulties in young children.* Committee on the Prevention of Reading Difficulties in Young Children. C.E. Snow, M.S. Burns, and P. Griffin, Eds. Commission on Behavioral and Social Sciences and Education. Washington, DC: National Academy Press.

National Research Council. (1999a). *The changing nature of work: Implications for occupational analysis.* Committee on Techniques for the Enhancement of Human Performance : Occupational Analysis. Commission on Behavioral and Social Sciences and Education. Washington, DC: National Academy Press.

National Research Council. (1999b). *Evaluating federal research programs: Research and the Government Performance and Results Act.* Committee on Science, Engineering, and Public Policy. National Academy of Sciences, National Academy of Engineering, Institute of Medicine. Washington, DC: National Academy Press.

National Research Council. (1999c). *How people learn: Brain, mind, experience, and school.* Committee on Developments in the Science of Learning. J.D. Bransford, A.L. Brown, and R.R. Cocking, Eds. Commission on Behavioral and Social Sciences and Education. Washington, DC: National Academy Press.

National Research Council. (1999d). *Improving student learning: A strategic plan for education research and its utilization.* Committee on a Feasibility Study for a Strategic Education Research Program. Commission on Behavioral and Social Sciences and Education. Washington, DC: National Academy Press.

National Research Council. (2001a). *Knowing and learning mathematics for teaching: Proceedings of a workshop.* Mathematics Teacher Preparation Content Workshop Program Steering Committee. Mathematical Sciences Education Board. Center for Education. Division of Behavioral and Social Sciences and Education. Washington, DC: National Academy Press.

National Research Council. (2001b). *Knowing what students know: The science and design of educational assessment.* Committee on the Foundations of Assessment. J. Pellegrino, N. Chudowsky, and R. Glaser, Eds. Center for Education. Division of Behavioral and Social Sciences and Education. Washington, DC: National Academy Press.

National Research Council. (2001c). *Observations on the President's Fiscal Year 2002 Federal Science and Technology Budget.* Committee on Science, Engineering, and Public Policy. National Academy of Sciences, National Academy of Engineering, Institute of Medicine. Washington, DC: National Academy Press.

National Research Council. (2001d). *Science, evidence, and inference in education: Report of a workshop.* Committee on Scientific Principles in Education Research. L. Towne, R.J. Shavelson, and M.J. Feuer, Eds. Center for Education. Division of Behavioral and Social Sciences and Education. Washington, DC: National Academy Press.

Nelson, R. (2000). Knowledge and innovation systems. In Organisation for Economic Co-Operation and Development (Ed.), *Knowledge management in the learning society* (pp. 115-124). Paris: Organisation for Economic Co-Operation and Development.

Newton-Smith, W.H. (1981). *The rationality of science.* London: Routledge.

Newton-Smith, W.H. (2000). *A companion to the philosophy of science.* Malden, MA: Blackwell.

Odden, A. (1990). Class size and student achievement: Research-based policy alternatives. *Educational Evaluation and Policy Analysis, 12*(2), 213-227.

Olson, R.K. (1999). Genes, environment, and reading disabilities. In R.J. Sternberg and L. Spear-Swerling (Eds.), *Perspectives on learning disabilities* (pp. 3-22). Oxford: Westview Press

Olson, R.K., Forsberg, H., Gayan, J., and DeFries, J.C. (1999). A behavioral-genetic analysis of reading disabilities and component processes. In R.M. Klein and P.A. McMullen (Eds.), *Converging methods for understanding reading and dyslexia* (pp. 133-153). Cambridge Mass.: MIT Press.

Orr, L.L. (1999). *Social experiments: Evaluating public programs with experimental methods.* Thousand Oaks, CA; Sage.

Packer, A. (1997). Mathematical competencies employers expect. In L. Steen (Ed.), *Why numbers count: Quantitative literacy for tomorrow's America* (pp. 137-154). New York: The College Board.

Palinscar, A.S., and Brown, A.L. (1984). Reciprocal teaching of comprehension-fostering and monitoring activities. *Cognition and Instruction, 1*(2), 117-135.

Paradise, J.L., Bluestone, C.D., Colborn, D.K., Bernard, B.S., Smith, C.G., Rockette, H.E., and Kurs-Lasky, M. (1999). Adenoidectomy and adenotonsillectomy for recurrent acute otitis media: Parallel randomized clinical trials in children not previously treated with tympanostomy tubes. *Journal of the American Medical Association (JAMA), 282*(10), 945-953.

Peltonen, L., and McKusick, V.A. (2001). Dissecting human disease in the postgenomic era. *Science, 291*(5507), 1224-1227, 1229.

Pennington, B.F. (1999). Dyslexia as a neurodevelopmental disorder. In H. Tager-Flusberg (Ed.), *Neurodevelopmental disorders* (pp. 307-330). Cambridge, MA: MIT Press.

Peterson, P.E. (1998). School choice: A report card. *Virginia Journal of Social Policy & the Law, 6*(1), 47-80.

Peterson, P.E., Howell, W.G., and Greene, J.P. (1999). An evaluation of the Cleveland voucher program after two years. Program on Education Policy and Governance Research Paper. Kennedy School of Government, Harvard University. Available: http://www.ksg.harvard.edu/pepg/. [2001, August 21].

Peterson, P.E., Myers, D., and Howell, W.G. (1999). *An evaluation of the Horizon Scholarship Program in the Edgewood Independent School District, San Antonio, Texas: The first year.* Washington, DC: Mathematica Policy Research.

Phillips, D. (1987). Validity in quantitative research, or, why the worry about warrant will not wane. *Education and Urban Society, 20*(1), 9-24.

Phillips, D. (2000). *The expanded social scientist's bestiary: A guide to fabled threats to, and defenses of, naturalistic social science.* Lanham, MD: Rowman & Littlefield.

Phillips, D., and Burbules, N.C. (2000). *Postpositivism and educational research.* Lanham, MD: Rowman & Littlefield.

Pieterse, M.E., Seydel, E.R., DeVries, H., Mudde, A.N., and Kok, G.J. (2001). Effectiveness of a minimal contact smoking cessation program for Dutch general practitioners: A randomized controlled trial. *Preventive Medicine, 32*(2), 182-190.

Polanyi, M. (1958). *Personal knowledge: Towards a post-critical philosophy.* Chicago: University of Chicago Press.

Pope, M.C., and Giles, K.A. (2001). Solid earth: Carbonate sediments. *Geotimes, 46*(7), 20-21.

Popper, K.R. (1959). *The logic of scientific discovery.* New York: Basic Books.

Popper, K.R. (1965). *Conjectures and refutations.* New York: Basic Books.

President's Committee of Advisors on Science and Technology. (1997). *Report to the President on the use of technology to strengthen K-12 education in the United States.* Available: http://www.ostp.gov/PCAST/k-12ed.html. [2001, August 21].

Puglisi, T. (2001). IRB review: It helps to know the regulatory framework. *APS Observer, 14*(5), 34-36.

Putnam, R.D. (1995). Bowling alone: America's declining social capital. *Journal of Democracy, 6,* 65-78.

Putnam, R.D., Leonardi, R., and Nanetti, R. (1993). *Making democracy work: Civic traditions in modern Italy.* Princeton, NJ: Princeton University Press.

Rasch, G. (1960). Probabilistic models for some intelligence and attainment tests. Originally published by the Denmarks Paedagogiske Institut. Republished in 1980 by the University of Chicago Press.

Reimers, F., and McGinn, N. (1997). *Informed dialog: Using research to shape education policy around the world.* Westport, CT: Praeger.

Ritter, G.W., and Boruch, R.F. (1999). The political and institutional origins of a randomized controlled trial on elementary school class size: Tennessee's Project STAR. *Educational Evaluation and Policy Analysis, 21*(2), 111-125.

Robinson, G.E., and Wittebols, J.H. (1986). *Class size research: A related cluster analysis for decision making.* Arlington, VA: Educational Research Service Inc.

Rogers, E.M. (1995). *Diffusion of innovations* (4th ed.). New York: Free Press.

Rosenbaum, P.R. (1995). *Observational studies.* New York: Springer-Verlag.

Rosenbaum, P.R., and Rubin, D.B. (1983). The central role of the propensity score in observational studies for causal effects. *Biometrika, 70,* 41-55.

Rosenbaum, P.R., and Rubin, D.B. (1984). Reducing bias in observational studies using subclassification on the propensity score. *Journal of the American Statistical Association, 79,* 516-524.

Roth, W-M. (2001). Learning science through technological design. *Journal of Research in Science Teaching, 38*(7), 768-790.

Rouse, C.E. (1997). Market approaches to education: Vouchers and school choice. *Economics of Education Review, 19*(4), 458-459.

RPP International. (2000). *The state of charter schools fourth-year report.* Washington, DC: U.S. Department of Education, Office of Educational Research and Improvement.

Rutter, M., Maughan, B., Mortimore, P., Ousten,, J., and Smith, A. (1979). *Fifteen thousand hours. Secondary schools and their effects on children.* Cambridge, MA: Harvard University Press.

Satz, P., and Fletcher, J.M. (1980). Minimal brain dysfunctions: An appraisal of research concepts and methods. In H. Rie and E. Rie (Eds.), *Handbook of minimal brain dysfunctions: A critical view* (pp. 669-715). New York: Wiley Interscience Series.

Schacter, J. (2001). *Geographical mobility: March 1999 to March 2000.* Current Population Reports. Washington, DC: U.S. Census Bureau, U.S. Department of Commerce.

Schmidt, M.A. (2001). Testimony to the U.S. House Committee on Education and the Workforce. 107th Cong., 1st Sess.

Schoenfeld, A.H. (1999). The core, the canon, and the development of research skills: Issues in the preparation of education researchers. In E.C. Lagemann and L. Shulman (Eds.), *Issues in education research.* San Francisco: Jossey-Bass.

Schoenfeld, A.H. (in press). Research methods in (mathematics) education. In L. English (Ed.), *International handbook of mathematics education.* Hillsdale, NJ: Lawrence Erlbaum Associates.

Schulte, T., Mattern, R., Berger, K., Syzmanksi, S., Klotz, P., Kraus, P.H., and Schols, L. (2001). Double-blind crossover trial of trimethoprim-sulfamethoxazole in spinocerebellar ataxia type 3/Machado-Joseph disease. *Archives of Neurology, 58*(9), 1451-1457.

Schum, D.A. (1994). *Evidential foundations of probabilistic reasoning.* New York: J. Wiley.

Secretary's Commission on Achieving Necessary Skills, U.S. Department of Labor. (1991). *What work requires of schools. A SCANS report for America 2000.* Washington, DC: U.S. Department of Labor.

Seymour, E. and Hewitt, N. (1997). *Talking about leaving: Why undergraduates leave the sciences.* Boulder, CO: Westview Press.

Shackleton, N.J. (2001). The 100,000-year ice-age cycle identified and found to lag temperature, carbon dioxide, and orbital eccentricity. *Science, 289,* 1897-1902.

Shankweiler, D.P. (1991). The contribution of Isabelle Y. Liberman. In S.A. Brady and D.P. Shankweiler (Eds.), *Phonological processes in literacy* (pp. xiii- xvii). Hillsdale NJ: Lawrence Erlbaum Associates.

Shavelson, R.J. (1988). Contributions of educational research to policy and practice: Constructing, challenging, changing cognition. *Educational Researcher, 17*(7), 4-11.

Shavelson, R.J. (1991). AERA's research and training grant. *Educational Researcher, 20*(9), 19-20.

Shavelson, R.J., Baxter, G.P., and Gao, X. (1993). Sampling variability of performance assessments. *Journal of Educational Measurement, 30*(3), 215-232.

Shavelson, R.J., and Berliner, D.C. (1988). Erosion of the education research infrastructure. *Educational Researcher, 17*(1), 9-12.

Shavelson, R., Feuer, M., and Towne, L. (2001, April). A scientific basis for educational research? Themes and lessons from a workshop. In *Education research planning at the National Research Council.* Symposium conducted at the annual meeting of the American Educational Research Association, Seattle, Washington.

Shaywitz, S. E. (1996). Dyslexia. *Scientific American, 275,* 98-104.

Shaywitz, S.E., Escobar, M.D., Shaywitz, B.A., Fletcher, J.M., and Makuch, R. (1992). Distribution and temporal stability of dyslexia in an epidemiological sample of 414 children followed longitudinally. *New England Journal of Medicine, 326,* 145-150.

Sheldon, E.B. (1975). The social indicators movement. In D.R. Krathwohl (Ed.), *Educational indicators: Monitoring the state of education.* Princeton: Educational Testing Service.

Shulman, L. (1997). Disciplines of inquiry in education: A new overview. In R. Jaeger (Ed.), *Complementary methods for research in education* (2nd ed., pp. 3-29). Washington, DC: American Educational Research Association.

Silverman, D. (1993). *Interpreting qualitative data: Methods for analyzing talk, text, and interaction.* London: Sage.

Skinner, B.F. (1953/1965). *Science and human behavior.* New York: Free Press.

Skinner, B.F. (1972). *Beyond freedom and dignity.* New York: Knopf.

Skocpol, T. (1996). Unravelling from above. *The American Prospect, 25,* 20-25.

Slavin, R. (1989). Class size and student achievement: Small effects of small classes. *Educational Psychologist, 24,* 99-110.

Smelser, N. (2001). How do the social sciences learn. Manuscript in preparation. Department of Sociology, University of California, Berkeley.

Spearman, C. (1904a). 'General intelligence' objectively determined and measured. *American Journal of Psychology, 15,* 201-293.

Spearman, C. (1904b). The proof and measurement of association between two things. *American Journal of Psychology, 15*, 72-101.

Spearman, C. (1910). Correlation calculated from faulty data. *British Journal of Psychology, 3*, 271-295.

Sroufe, G.E. (1997). Improving the "awful reputation" of education research. *Educational Researcher, 26*(7), 26-28.

Stanovich, K.E. (1991). The psychology of reading: Evolutionary and revolutionary devleopments. *Annual Review of Applied Linguistics, 12*, 3-30.

Stanovich, K.E. (2000). *Progress in understanding reading: Scientific foundations and new frontiers.* New York: Guilford.

Stecher, B.M., and Bohrnstedt, G.W. (Eds.). (2000). Class size reduction in California: Summary of the 1998-99 evaluation findings. CSR Research Consortium Year 2 Evaluation Report. Sacramento, CA: California Department of Education.

Stedman, L.C. (1985). A new look at the effective schools literature. *Urban Education, 20*(3).

Steffe, L., and Thompson, P. (2000). Teaching experiment methodology: Underlying principles and essential elements. In A.E. Kelly and R. Lesh (Eds.), *Handbook of research design in mathematics and science education* (pp. 267-306). Mahwah, NJ: Lawrence Erlbaum Associates.

Stokes, D.E. (1997). *Pasteur's quadrant: Basic science and technological innovation.* Washington, DC: Brookings Institution Press.

Thorndike, R.L. (1949). *Personnel selection: Test and measurement techniques.* New York: Wiley.

Thurstone, L.L. (1931). Multiple factor analysis. *Psychological Review, 38,* 406-427.

Trant, J.D. (1991). Reductionism and the unity of science. In R. Boyd, P. Gasper, and J.D. Trant (Eds.), *The philosophy of science.* Cambridge, MA: Bradford Books/MIT Press.

Tucker, W.H. (1994). Fact and fiction in the discovery of Sir Cyril Burt's flaws. *Journal of the History of the Behavioral Sciences, 30*(4), 335-347.

Tyack, D., and Cuban, L. (1995). *Tinkering toward utopia: A century of public school reform.* Cambridge, MA: Harvard University Press.

U.S. Government Accounting Office. (1999). *Federal research: Peer review practices at federal agencies vary.* Report to Congressional Requesters. Washington, DC: Author.

U.S. Department of Education. (2000). *The nation's report card: Mathematics 2000,* NCES 2001–517, by J.S. Braswell, A.D. Lutkus, W.S. Grigg, S.L. Santapau, B. Tay-Lim, and M. Johnson. Washington, DC: Office of Educational Research and Improvement, National Center for Education Statistics, U.S. Department of Education.

Vellutino, F.R. (1979). *Dyslexia: Theory and research*. Cambridge, MA: MIT Press.

Vinovskis, M.A. (2000). The federal role in educational research and development. In D. Ravitch (Ed.), *Brookings papers on education policy* (pp. 359-380). Washington, DC: Brookings Institution Press.

Wagner, R.K., Torgesen, J.K., and Rashotte, C.A. (1994). Development of reading-related phonological processing abilities: New evidence of bidirectional causality from a latent variable longitudinal study. *Developmental Psychology, 30*(1), 73-87.

Watson, J.D., and Crick, F. (1953). Molecular structure of nucleic acids: A structure for deoxyribose nucleic acid. *Nature (London, England), 171*(2), 737-738.

Webb, E., Campbell, D., Schwartz, R. and Sechrest, L. (1966). *Unobtrusive measures: Nonreactive research in the social sciences*. Chicago: Rand McNally.

Weiss, C.H. (1991a). Knowledge creep and decision accretion. In D.S. Anderson and B.J. Biddle (Eds.), *Knowledge for policy: Improving education through research* (pp. 183-192). London: Falmer Press.

Weiss, C.H. (1991b). The many meanings of research utilization. In D.S. Anderson and B.J. Biddle (Eds.), *Knowledge for policy: Improving education through research* (pp. 173-182). London: Falmer Press.

Weiss, C.H. (1995). The four "I's" of school reform: How interests, ideology, information, and institution affect teachers and principals. *Harvard Educational Review, 65*(4), 571-592.

Weiss, C.H. (1998a). *Evaluation: Methods for studying programs and policies*. Upper Saddle River, NJ: Prentice Hall.

Weiss, C.H. (1998b). Improving the use of evaluations: Whose job is it anyway? In A.J. Reynolds and H.J. Walberg (Eds.), *Advances in educational productivity* (pp. 263-276). Stamford, CT: JAI Press.

Weiss, C.H. (1999). Research-policy linkages: How much influence does social science research have? In *UNESCO, world social science report 1999* (pp. 194-205). Paris: UNESCO/Elsevier.

Weiss, C.H. (in press). What to do until the random assigner comes. In F. Mosteller and R. Boruch (Eds.), *Evidence matters: Randomized trials in education research*. Washington, DC: Brookings Institution Press.

Weiss, C.H. (with Bucuvalas, M.J.). (1980). *Social science research and decision-making*. New York: Columbia University Press.

Willinsky, J. (2001). The strategic education research program and the public value of research. *Educational Researcher, 30*(1), 5-14.

Wilson, E.O. (1998). *Consilience*. New York: Vintage Books.

Winograd, I.J., Coplen, T.B., and Landwehr, J.M. (1992). Continuous 500,000-year climate record from vein calcite in Devils Hole, Nevada. *Science, 258*, 255-260.

Winter, I. (2000). Major themes and debates in the social capital literature: The Australian connection. In I. Winter (Ed.), *Social capital and public policy in Australia*. Melbourne, Australia: Australian Institute of Family Studies.

Wissler, C. (1901). The correlation of mental and physical traits. *Psychological Review. Monograph Supplement, 3*(6).

Witte, J.F. (2000). *The market approach to education: An analysis of America's first voucher program*. Princeton, NJ: Princeton University Press.

Wittgenstein, L. (1968). *Philosophical investigations* (Trans. G.E.M. Ansombe) (3rd ed.). New York: Macmillan.

Word, E., Johnston, J., Bain, H.P., Fulton, B.D., Zaharias, J. B., Achilles, C.M., Lintz, M.N., Folger, J., and Breda, C. (1990). *The state of Tennessee's Student/Teacher Achievement Ratio (STAR) Project: Final summary report 1985-1990*. Nashville, TN: Tennessee Department of Education.

Yin, R.K. (2000). Rival explanations as an alternative to reforms as 'experiments.' In L. Bickman (Ed.), *Validity and social experimentation: Donald Campbell's legacy* (pp. 239-266). Thousand Oaks, CA: Sage.

Yin, R.K., and White, J.L. (1986). *Managing for excellence in urban high schools: District and school roles. Final report*. Washington, DC: Office of Educational Research and Improvement, U.S. Department of Education.

Ziman, J.M. (2000). *Real science: What it is, and what it means*. New York: Cambridge University Press.

APPENDIX

Biographical Sketches, Committee Members and Staff

Donald I. Barfield is deputy director at WestEd, a nonprofit research, development, and service agency dedicated to improving education and other opportunities for children, youth, and adults. As a deputy director, Mr. Barfield is responsible for overseeing all research and development, evaluation, and technical assistance proposals from WestEd and for developing new lines of work within the agency, acquisitions, and key business partnerships. In addition to his work in leading WestEd's resource development and strategic planning efforts, he supervises WestEd's mathematics and science program, the National Center for Improving Science Education, and the technology in education program. Mr. Barfield has presented testimony before Congress on student assessment issues and the use of test data in schools, has participated as a contractor and advisor to the California State Department of Education on statewide assessment and accountability systems since 1989 and is currently a court-appointed expert in the San Francisco Unified School District's desegregation case. Previously, he helped develop and establish the Bay Area Annenberg Project, directed Far West Laboratory's Center for Teaching and Learning, and served as assistant superintendent for research, testing, and evaluation in the San Francisco Unified School District. He earned an M.A. in sociology from Harvard University.

Robert F. Boruch is university chair professor in the Graduate School of Education and the Statistics Department of the Wharton School at the

University of Pennsylvania. A fellow of the American Statistical Association, he has received awards for his work on research methods and policy from the American Educational Research Association, the American Evaluation Association, and the Policy Studies Association. He is the author of nearly 150 scholarly papers and author or editor of a dozen books on topics ranging from evaluation of AIDS prevention programs and social experiments to assuming confidentiality of data in social research. His most recent book is titled *Randomized Experiments for Planning and Evaluation: A Practical Guide,* 1997, published by Sage. He earned a Ph.D. in psychology from Iowa State University.

Jere Confrey is professor of education, University of Texas at Austin. She directs the Systemic Research Collaborative for Mathematics, Science, and Technology (SYRCE) and cofounded the UTeach teacher preparation program for grades 4-12. She is vice chair of the Mathematical Sciences Education Board of the National Academy of Sciences. She was the founder of the SummerMath program for young women at Mount Holyoke College and cofounder of SummerMath for Teachers. Her research focuses on urban school reform, systemic change models, and children's understanding of multiplication, division, ratio and trigonometry. She is coauthor of the software Function Probe, Class Tab, and of sets of interactive diagrams for illustrating core mathematical ideas. She has served as vice president of the International Group for the Psychology of Mathematics Education, chair of the SIG-Research in Mathematics Education, and on the editorial boards of the *Journal for Research in Mathematics Educational* and the *International Journal for Computers in Mathematics Learning.* She has been a member of the Department of Education's Expert Panel on Technology, and has taught school at the elementary, secondary, and postsecondary levels. She received a Ph.D. in mathematics education from Cornell University.

Rudolph Crew is the director of school reform initiatives at the Stupski Family Foundation in Mill Valley, California. He previously served as the first executive director of the University of Washington's new Institute for K-12 Leadership, and affiliate professor of leadership and policy studies in the College of Education. Prior to joining the University of Washington, Crew was chancellor of New York Public Schools for 4 years. He has also served as superintendent of the Tacoma Public Schools and the Sacramento

City Unified School District and has held various other teaching and administrative positions in California and Boston. He holds M.A. and Ed.D. degrees from the University of Massachusetts, Amherst.

Robert L. DeHaan is professor of cell biology, emeritus at Emory Medical School and adjunct professor in the Division of Educational Studies at Emory University. He currently directs a precollege science education effort, the Elementary Science Education Partners (ESEP) Program, which supplies undergraduate "science partners" and professional development to elementary teachers of the Atlanta Public School and neighboring Fulton County school districts. Previously, he was on the faculties of the Carnegie Institution of Washington, the Johns Hopkins University, and the Emory School of Medicine, focusing on the biophysical differentiation of the embryonic heart. He has published two books and over 100 research papers in cellular science and embryology, and he has trained over 40 graduate students and post-doctoral fellows. In 1998 he received the first Bruce Alberts Award from the American Society of Cell Biologists for distinguished contributions to science education. In addition to his work in bench science and precollege education, he founded and was the first director of the Emory Center for Ethics in Public Policy and the Professions and is now faculty scholar at the Center. He received a Ph.D. from the University of California at Los Angeles.

Margaret Eisenhart is professor of educational anthropology and research methodology in the School of Education, University of Colorado at Boulder. Previously, she taught at the College of Education at Virginia Tech. Her research and publications have focused on bringing the perspective of anthropology to bear on current U.S. educational issues, including most notably the influences of gender and ethnicity on educational experiences and achievement. She has also written extensively about applications of ethnographic research methods in educational research. She is coauthor of three books and author or co-author of more than 50 articles and chapters. She founded and directs the Center for Youth in Science, Culture and NewMedia (cy.Scan) at the University of Colorado. She received a Ph.D. in anthropology from the University of North Carolina at Chapel Hill.

Jack McFarlin Fletcher is a professor in the Department of Pediatrics at the University of Texas-Houston Health Science Center and associate director of the Center for Academic and Reading Skills. He previously directed the School Problems Clinic at the University of Texas-Houston. For the past 20 years, Dr. Fletcher, a child neuropsychologist, has completed research on many aspects of the development of reading, language, and other cognitive skills in children. He has worked extensively on issues related to learning and attention problems, including definition and classification, neurobiological correlates, intervention, and, most recently, the development of literacy skills in Spanish-speaking children and bilingual children. He served on and chaired the mental retardation/developmental disabilities study section of the National Institute for Child Health and Human Development and is a former member of its maternal and child health study section. He chaired a committee on children with persistent reading disability for the Houston Independent School District (HISD) and served on a task force on reading for HISD. He earned a Ph.D. in clinical psychology from the University of Florida.

Eugene E. Garcia is professor of education at the University of California, Berkeley. He previously served as a faculty member at the University of Utah; the University of California, Santa Barbara; Arizona State University; and the University of California, Santa Cruz. He has served previously as a national research center director and as an academic department chair and dean. He has published extensively in the area of language teaching and bilingual development, authoring or coauthoring over 150 articles and book chapters, along with eight book-length volumes. He served as a senior officer and director of the Office of Bilingual Education and Minority Languages Affairs in the U.S. Department of Education from 1993 to 1995, and is conducting research in the area of effective schooling for linguistically and culturally diverse student populations. He received a B.A. from the University of Utah in psychology, and a Ph.D. in human development from the University of Kansas.

Norman Hackerman is chairman of the Scientific Advisory Board at the Robert A. Welch Foundation and president emeritus and distinguished professor emeritus of chemistry at Rice University. He spent 25 years at The University of Texas, Austin, where he joined the faculty as an assistant professor of chemistry in 1945 and progressed to president in 1967. He taught chemistry at Loyola College and Virginia Tech, and worked as a research chemist for Colloid Corporation, Kellex Corporation, and the U.S. Coast Guard. He was a member of the National Science Board from 1968 to 1980, and its chairman from 1975 to 1980. He was the editor of the *Journal of the Electrochemical Society* from 1969 to 1989. He is a member of the National Academy of Sciences, the American Philosophical Society, and the American Academy of Arts and Sciences, as well as numerous scientific organizations. He is author or coauthor of 226 publications. He has served on the NRC's Committee on Science Education K-12 since 1996, and is also a member of its Science and Technology Editorial Board. He received a B.A. and a Ph.D. from Johns Hopkins University.

Eric Hanushek is the Paul and Jean Hanna senior fellow on education policy at the Hoover Institution of Stanford University and a research associate of the National Bureau of Economic Research. His research concentrates on applied public finance and public policy analysis with special emphasis on education issues. He had prior academic appointments at the University of Rochester, Yale University, and the U.S. Air Force Academy. From 1983 to 1985, he was deputy director of the Congressional Budget Office. He has published numerous books, including *Making Schools Work: Improving Performance and Controlling Costs*, and articles on a variety of subjects in professional journals. He has a Ph.D. in economics from the Massachusetts Institute of Technology.

Robert Hauser is Vilas research professor and Samuel A. Stouffer professor of Sociology at the University of Wisconsin-Madison. His current research includes the Wisconsin Longitudinal Study—a study of aging, the life course, and social stratification—and is also studying national trends and differentials in educational attainment, school dropout, and grade retention. He is a member of the National Academy of Sciences and of the National Academy of Education. He served as co-principal investigator on the NRC evaluation of the Voluntary National Tests and chaired the Committee on Appropriate Uses of High Stakes Tests. He received a B.A. in economics from the University of Chicago and M.A. and Ph.D. degrees in sociology from the University of Michigan.

Paul W. Holland is the Frederick M. Lord chair in measurement and statistics at the Educational Testing Service in Princeton, NJ. Prior to rejoining ETS in 2000, he was professor in the Graduate School of Education and Department of Statistics at the University of California, Berkeley. He is a member of the NRC's Board on Testing and Assessment, and has served on the Design and Analysis Committee for the National Assessment of Educational Progress and as an advisor to the California Commission on Teacher Credentialing. He chaired the NRC panel on Equivalency and Linkage of Educational Tests. His research interests include applications of statistics to the social and behavioral sciences, the analysis of categorical data, causal inference in non-experimental research, psychometrics, latent variable models, and test linking. His contributions to psychometrics include a book on test equating and another on differential item functioning. He is a fellow of the American Statistical Association, the Institute of Mathematical Statistics, and the American Association for the Advancement of Science. He is a past president of the Psychometric Society and in 2000 he was awarded the American Educational Research Association/American College Testing Program's E.F. Lindquist Award. He earned an M.S. and a Ph.D. in statistics from Stanford University.

Ellen Condliffe Lagemann is president of the Spencer Foundation and on leave as professor of history and education at New York University. An historian of education, her professional life has been devoted to investigation of the field of educational research and of philanthropy. She is the author or editor of nine books and countless reviews. Her most recent book, published by the University of Chicago Press in 2000, is *An Elusive Science: The Troubling History of Education Research*. Before joining the faculty of New York University as director of the Center for the Study of American Culture and Education and chair of the Department of Humanities and the Social Sciences in the School of Education, she taught at Teachers College and in the Department of History at Columbia University. She is a member of the National Academy of Education and has served as its president since 1998. Formerly, she was president of the History of Education Society, vice chair of the Board of Directors of the Center for Advanced Study in the Behavioral Sciences, and a board member of the Greenwall Foundation in New York City. In addition, she currently serves on the board of the Markle and Russell Sage Foundations. A graduate of Smith College, she taught high school in New York before receiving an M.A. from Teachers College, Columbia University, and a Ph.D. from Columbia University.

Denis C. Phillips is professor of education and (by courtesy) professor of philosophy at Stanford University, where he served as the School of Education's associate dean for academic affairs from 1994 to 2001. Trained initially as a biologist and science teacher, he moved into philosophy of social science and the history of nineteenth and twentieth century thought, especially as it concerns the emergence of the biological and social sciences. He is a fellow of the International Academy of Education, a past president of the Philosophy of Education Society, and was a section editor of the *International Encyclopedia of Education* (2nd ed). His recent work has been focussed on defending the possibility of scientifically rigorous educational research in the light of contemporary criticisms; and he has given workshops on topics in philosophy of science for educational researchers in a number of countries worldwide. He also has been working on an analysis of constructivist thought in education, psychology, and philosophy. He has authored, coauthored, or edited 10 books and more than 100 journal articles and book and encyclopedia chapters. He has a Ph.D in philosophy of science and philosophy of education from the University of Melbourne in Australia.

Richard J. Shavelson (chair) is a professor in the School of Education and the Department of Psychology (by courtesy) at Stanford University, and past dean of the School of Education. He is a member of the National Academy of Education and a fellow of the American Association for the Advancement of Science, the American Psychological Association, the American Psychological Society, and the Center for Advanced Studies in the Behavioral Sciences. For more than 20 years, he has sought new techniques for measuring performance in ways that contribute to educational and workplace goals, exploring, for example, alternatives to multiple-choice tests in schools, on the job, and in the military. His recent research has focused on new assessment tools for science and mathematics achievement, measuring individual and group performance in science and mathematics;

statistically modeling performance assessment; and addressing policy and practice issues in measurement reform. He has chaired the NRC's Board on Testing and Assessment. As professor of education and psychology at Stanford and as the dean of the School of Education, he implemented a wide-range plan for the school; created partnerships with the Stanford schools of business, law, engineering, and humanities and sciences; and increased links between the school and the local education and business communities. He has published several books, monographs, and more than 100 articles, reports, and chapters. He received a Ph.D. in educational psychology from Stanford University in 1971.

Lisa Towne is a senior program officer in the NRC's Center for Education and adjunct instructor of quantitative methods at Georgetown University's Public Policy Institute. She has also worked for the White House Office of Science and Technology Policy and the U.S. Department of Education Planning and Evaluation Service. She received an M.P.P. from Georgetown University.

Carol H. Weiss is the Beatrice S. Whiting professor at the Harvard Graduate School of Education, where she teaches in the area of administration, planning, and social policy. Her courses include evaluation methods, research methods, using research as a strategy of change, and organizational decision making. She has published 11 books on evaluation and the uses of research and evaluation in policy making and more than 100 articles and book chapters. Her publications have been translated into German, French, Spanish, Portuguese, Thai, and Ukrainian. Her recent work is about the influences on educational policy making from ideology, interests, information, and institutional constraints. She has been a fellow at the Center for Advanced Study in the Behavioral Sciences, a guest scholar at the Brookings Institution, a congressional fellow under the sponsorship of the American Sociological Association, a senior fellow at the U.S. Department of Education, and a member of several NRC panels. She is on editorial boards for *Teachers College Record*, the *Journal of Educational Change*, *Journal of Comparative Policy Analysis*, *Asia-Pacific Journal of Teacher Education and Development*, *American Behavioral Scientist*, and others. She holds a Ph.D. in sociology from Columbia University.